*The*

# WINE SAVANT

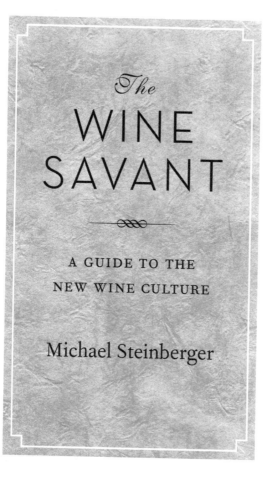

*The*

# WINE
# SAVANT

## A GUIDE TO THE
## NEW WINE CULTURE

Michael Steinberger

W. W. NORTON & COMPANY

New York   London

For information about permission to reproduce selections from this book,
write to Permissions, W. W. Norton & Company, Inc.,
500 Fifth Avenue, New York, NY 10110

For information about special discounts for bulk purchases, please contact
W. W. Norton Special Sales at specialsales@wwnorton.com or 800-233-4830

Manufacturing by Courier Westford
Book design by Cassandra Pappas
Production manager: Devon Zahn

Library of Congress Cataloging-in-Publication Data

Steinberger, Michael.
The wine savant : a guide to the new wine culture / Michael Steinberger. — First edition.
    pages cm
Includes index.
ISBN 978-0-393-08271-5 (hardcover)
1. Wine and wine making. I. Title.
    TP548.S72174 2013
    663'.2—dc23
                                    2013031572

W. W. Norton & Company, Inc.
500 Fifth Avenue, New York, N.Y. 10110
www.wwnorton.com

W. W. Norton & Company Ltd.
Castle House, 75/76 Wells Street, London W1T 3QT

1 2 3 4 5 6 7 8 9 0

*To Kathy, James, and Ava*
*(and Patches, too)*

# Contents

# WINE SAVANT

# Introduction

ℐN 2004, Fox Searchlight released a low-budget movie called *Sideways*, about a bachelor weekend in California wine country. The main character, Miles Raymond, played by Paul Giamatti, was a struggling, chronically depressed writer who also happened to be an insufferable wine snob. Visiting one winery, Miles theatrically dipped his nose in the glass and claimed to smell the faintest "soupçon of asparagus" and a "flutter of a nutty Edam cheese." Oenophiles in the theater cringed in embarrassment—for him, for us. Wine buffs are nothing if not self-conscious, and here was a major motion picture trafficking in the worst stereotypes about wine appreciation, presenting it as a hobby full of absurd rituals and pretentious blather, pursued mainly by pompous twits. The pessimists in our ranks feared that *Sideways* would set back the cause of oenophilia in America by at least a generation.

Twenty years earlier, that probably would have been the case. Back then, the United States was still solidly shot-and-beer territory, with a deep aversion to wine. In certain parts of the country, merely ordering a glass of Cabernet was enough to raise doubts about one's manhood and patriotism. But in the late 1990s, large numbers of Americans started to realize what the French, Italians, and Spanish had figured out centuries earlier: wine is a uniquely pleasurable libation and goes smashingly with food. By the time *Sideways* came out, the United States was in the midst of a wine-drinking revolution. Far from regarding Miles as an annoying alien, the audience embraced him as someone it could relate to. Sure, theatergoers laughed at his excesses and affectations, but they then ran out and took his wine advice. His famous dismissal of Merlot—"If anybody orders Merlot, I'm leaving; I'm *not* drinking any fucking Merlot!"—torpedoed sales of what had been America's most popular red wine, while his love of Pinot Noir touched off a Pinot craze, known as the "*Sideways* effect," which continues to this day.

A year after *Sideways* was released, a Gallup poll found that for the first time ever, Americans preferred wine to beer. Here was incontrovertible evidence that we had ceased to be a nation of oenophobes and had become a land of grape nuts. And so we are. America's wine consumption has more than doubled in the past fifteen years, and in 2011 the United States surpassed France in overall wine consumption. With the onset of the Great Recession, some observers were concerned that the interest in wine would flag—that Americans would stop drinking the fancy stuff and revert to beer or hard liquor. It didn't happen. While people cut back on what they were spending per bottle, wine sales did not decline, even during the worst months of the economic downturn, which was testament to how deep the oenophilia now ran. It is no exaggeration to say that New York and San Francisco have better wine scenes than you find in Paris these days. Our wine shops are bursting with compelling choices from around the world, and Americans have proven themselves to be among the most curious and ecumenical wine drinkers on the planet.

In fact, as wine goes, the United States has become the great savior, rescuing whole categories of wine from near-extinction or obsolescence. Take, for instance, traditional German Rieslings, which normally contain a certain amount of sweetness; these wines are now shunned by German consumers, who want their Rieslings bone dry. But over the past decade or so, the "fruity" style has found a very enthusiastic following in the United States; without the American market, the fruity genre would hardly exist now. A funny thing has happened: contradicting the idea that America is the death star of globalization, stamping out ancient practices wherever it finds them, the United States has become a safe harbor for all sorts of traditional wines. Along with their taste for fruity German Rieslings, American oenophiles are smitten with traditional Barolos and Barbarescos, classic Riojas, artisanal *cru* Beaujolais, Madeira, and Sherry—all wines that might otherwise be on the endangered species list. This speaks to the passion and sophistication of American wine drinkers. We no longer need to be sold on wine; the sale has been made, and a vibrant, self-confident wine culture has taken root in the United States.

Today Americans have a very different relationship with wine than they did fifteen years ago; the fear has lifted, the training wheels are off, and we have become a nation of wine drinkers. A new era requires a new kind of wine guide, one that both informs and entertains, that is tailored to people who enjoy wine, who like learning about it, and who'd love to get inside dope from someone immersed in the wine profession. *The Wine Savant* is a guidebook for this new era. It is not a typical, A–Z wine guide. There are plenty of those already on the market; we don't need another. Consider it instead an opinionated, highly idiosyncratic guide to parts of the wine world—parts I like, parts that interest me, parts that I enjoy writing about and that I hope you'll enjoy reading about. Those looking for a comprehensive rundown of, say, South American wines have come to the wrong place. Certainly some good wines are being made in Chile and Argentina; if the Chileans would back off on the use of new oak, I think they could do something special with Carmenere, the so-called

A transplanted French grape, Carmenere, has become Chile's signature variety, so it is perhaps only fitting that the finest wines coming out of Chile these days—some of the finest wines in all South America, in my opinion—are being made by a transplanted Frenchman. Louis-Antoine Luyt, a protégé of the late, venerated Beaujolais wine-maker Marcel Lapierre, is crafting sensational wines in the Maule region of Chile. His first project there was a winery cleverly called Clos Ouvert, and it was under that label that Luyt put out a truly amazing Carmenere—earthy, elegant, redolent of black olives and leather. The devastating earthquake that hit Chile in 2010 brought Clos Ouvert to a premature end, but Luyt is now making wines in Chile under his own name. The portfolio includes a Cinsault, a Carignan, and a couple of different cuvées using País, a grape that is believed to have been brought to South America in the sixteenth century and that at one time was Chile's main variety. These are delicious, distinctive wines that speak to both Luyt's talent and the potential that exists in Chile.

Lost Grape of Bordeaux (it disappeared from Bordeaux when the region was overrun by the phylloxera root louse in the late 1800s and was discovered flourishing in Chile a century later). But at the risk of insulting an entire continent—why not go big?—I can't think of many instances in which I've been drinking a South American wine and didn't wish that I were drinking something else. I'm optimistic that that will change, but in these pages I prefer to focus on regions whose wines and stories excite me the most and where I think I have the most insight to impart.

Consider *The Wine Savant* a polemical wine guide, combining practical advice with lots of opinion—it is both fish and fowl, you might say. It is above all an advice manual for how to think about wine, how to be a shrewd wine consumer, and how to maximize the pleasure that you get from wine. It opens with a spirited defense of oenophilia (despite wine's growing popularity, the age-old perception that it is a drink for snobs persists), then moves on to discuss becoming a wine maven, becoming a savvier wine buyer, and the eternally vexing question of food and wine pairings. There are also chapters about value wines and bucket-list wines, with lots of recommendations in both. What's the best wine region in California? (Hint: it's not Napa or Sonoma.) What's the difference between organic, biodynamic, and natural wines, and what the hell is a spoofulated wine? Which matters more, the vintage or the vintner? Are supertasters better tasters? Is the shape of a wineglass really that important? What's the first thing you should do upon entering a wine shop? These and many other questions are answered here.

Amid all the practical information, *The Wine Savant* examines all sorts of interesting and contentious issues related to wine. Are wine critics trustworthy? Why did California become a whipping boy for wine geeks, and why is it suddenly the Promised Land again? Why is Burgundy so fashionable and Bordeaux so passé? Why, contrary to expectations, has globalization proven to be a boon for obscure grapes and obscure wine regions?

There has never been a more exciting time to be a wine enthusiast, and in recent years oenophilia has swept the planet. Hong Kong has eclipsed New York and London as the world's richest wine auction market, and winemakers in Bordeaux, Napa, Barossa, and other places are now swooning over the Chinese market and its vast potential. India and Russia have caught the wine bug, too, as has Brazil. Suddenly collectors in Western Europe and America, who used to have the market for rare Burgundies and Bordeaux pretty much to themselves, are facing competition for prized bottles from newly minted oenophiles in Shanghai and Shenzhen. For some wines, such as Château Lafite-Rothschild, one of the five Bordeaux first growths, there is no competition: Asian buyers rule the market.

Fortunately, being priced out of a wine, or an even an entire class of wines, is now merely an invitation to discover new wines. The past fifteen years have also seen a quality explosion in the wine world. In the not-so-distant past, a reasonably savvy oenophile could put together a respectable cellar with wines from just a handful of places—Bordeaux, Burgundy, Champagne, Napa, the Mosel, the Douro—and a handful of grapes—Cabernet, Pinot Noir, Syrah, Chardonnay, Riesling. These days, however, compelling wines are being made in all sorts of unlikely and unfamiliar places (hello, Canary Islands!), and there has been an explosion in the number of grapes represented on American retail shelves. Alongside the Cabernets and Chardonnays, you now find Albariños, Verdejos, Grüner Veltliners, Aglianicos, Lagreins, Blaufränkisches, and many others. Better farming and winemaking practices, stepped-up competition—these are the primary factors that have driven this global quality revolution, and it is safe to say that there has never been a better time to be a wine drinker.

But there has also never been a more confusing time to be one. With so many different wines made from so many different grapes hailing from so many different regions, the choices can be overwhelming. Plus, thanks to the Internet, there's now a cacophony of critics, professional and amateur alike, lauding wines, lambasting wines, and so on. Wine may be a simple pleasure, but it is also a complex beverage, and never more so than now. In 2012, *Wine Spectator* columnist Matt Kramer wrote a piece in which he talked about the democratization of wine enthusiasm—how oenophilia is today more accessible to far more people than ever before. But he added an important caveat. "The new wine democracy," he wrote, "is not about money, but rather how much effort you're willing to expend. Are you willing (and sufficiently interested) to read about and then hunt down all those thrilling little producers in the Loire Valley, in Spain, Portugal, Oregon, Greece, New Zealand, and the unheralded nooks and crannies of California? If you are—and you actually do it—you're in. Welcome to the wine elite."

That education process is part of the pleasure of wine, too. Like all alcoholic beverages, wine has the ability to make you feel happy; what sets it apart is its ability also to make you think. No other alcoholic drink—no other beverage, period—is as deeply rooted in the human experience as wine. Indeed, it has been integral to the human experience for more than two millennia, and combines history, politics, and culture in a way unmatched by any other potable. Just think about the present moment. Wine sits at the nexus of some of the most significant stories of our time—globalization, climate change, the rise of China. It turns out that wine, in addition to offering singular pleasure, is a pretty good lens through which to view our world. Take, for instance, the issue of counterfeit wines. In recent years the fine wine market has seen a surge in counterfeit rarities. It's a delicious story, with an international and very colorful cast of characters. It has produced one best-selling book (*The Billionaire's Vinegar*) and numerous magazine and newspaper articles and may yet yield a major motion picture (full disclosure: an article that I wrote for *Vanity Fair* in 2012 about the rise and fall of Rudy Kurniawan, who allegedly flooded the market with fake Bordeaux and Burgundies, was optioned for film rights).

But the onslaught of fake wines is part of a larger tale, about the global wealth boom of the past few decades and the tireless pursuit of cultural capital by the newly moneyed. Above all, what created a market for all these fake Lafites and Romanée-Contis was the desire of wealthy people to be able to say that they had experienced something unique, that their wealth had conferred on them the ability to taste the rarest of the rare—wines like the 1945 Romanée-Conti, of which just 608 bottles were produced and which has become a popular counterfeit item. A collector friend of mine once told me that with wines like the '45 Romanée-Conti, you quickly leave the realm of fermented grape juice and enter the deepest recesses of the mind. "You've paid a lot of money to experience the wine, and you're so emotionally invested in having this experience, in being able to say that you tasted the 'forty-five RC, that you can easily convince yourself that the wine is great even if it really isn't," he said. Those who manufactured fake rarities understood the psychology of their intended victims perfectly, and ultrawealthy collectors, so anxious to acquire that cultural capital, turned out to be shockingly easy marks.

For me, a big part of the pleasure of writing about wine is exploring the culture of oenophilia and connecting it to these broader themes. I think the finest wine writing combines helpful tips with insights into the people, places, politics, history, and economics of wine, and that's what I have attempted to do here. Many of my ideas are drawn from the nearly ten years I spent as the wine columnist for *Slate* magazine, the pioneering online journal, and some of the material is drawn from it, too. It wouldn't be quite accurate to say that *Slate* gave me the freedom to write about wine in a different style from that of other publications; the editors insisted on it, which was great, because I wanted to write about wine in a different way—I wanted the column to be punchy, entertaining, and slightly irreverent. I think it was all that, but it also helped steer readers to many exciting wines from around the world. You'll find the same combination of spirited wine talk and practical insights in these pages.

—⊶⊷—

# Wine Without Apologies

*I*T HAPPENS without fail every election season: at some point during the campaign, a candidate will be portrayed as being the favorite of wine-sipping elites. Sometimes the description is more specific: the candidate will be described as the choice of *Chardonnay*-sipping elites (as if Chardonnay is somehow more froufrou than other wines). Inevitably the candidate will be a Democrat, since everyone knows that only limp-wristed lefties enjoy wine, and political commentators will expound anew on America's wine versus beer divide. Get the impression that all this blather about wine and political allegiances drives me nuts? It does. The idea that alcohol preferences are linked to political allegiances is asinine. Worse, though, is the underlying premise—the notion that wine is something exotic and somehow alien to mainstream America, that it is a beverage that appeals only to decadent coastal elites who are more Continental than Yankee.

Warning: A rant is coming.

Maddeningly, this image of wine persists in American pop culture even though we have become a nation of wine enthusiasts. There is apparently no limit, for instance, to the media's enthusiasm for studies that cast doubt on wine connoisseurship. If a group of "experts" decides that they prefer a $10 wine to a $100 bottle, rest assured that the story will be headline news as soon as it breaks. That's especially true if the study involves some sort of ruse—say, switching the labels on the bottles. Poseurs humiliated! It is a mystery to me why these stories continue to hold so much appeal for reporters and editors, many of whom surely enjoy a glass of Muscadet or Mencia whenever it comes their way. No doubt a certain segment of the public—a small, shrinking, very sad segment—finds pleasure in such stories. But really, these efforts to paint wine appreciation as pretentious nonsense are woefully outdated.

So why do they persist? To a certain extent, we oenophiles invite the abuse (yes, I'm being dramatic for effect here). While a very self-confident wine culture—confident in its taste, receptive to all sorts of wines—has indeed taken root in the United States, we grape nuts don't do a good job of projecting that confidence. Quite the opposite: we seem to apologize for our oenophilia and continuously downplay wine's significance. I'm as guilty of this as anyone: I can't tell you how many times I've trotted out lines like "Wine isn't war and peace" or "It's only fermented grape juice." It's sort of a preemptive cringe. And what are we cringing from? Accusations of snobbery. Much of the public and private discussion of wine revolves around the notion that people who are wine enthusiasts are by definition snobs—that merely possessing a keen interest in wine and some knowledge of it marks you as a snob. Not surprisingly, wine writers, who communicate with a broad audience routinely, are particularly sensitive to this charge and tend to strike an apologetic or self-deprecatory note reflexively when it comes to their own expertise, so as to not be branded with the scarlet *S* (as in *Snob*). The shelves of bookstores are stuffed with wine guides that seek either to capitalize on the presumed link between wine connoisseurship and snootiness (*The Wine Snob's Dictionary, The Official Guide to Wine Snobbery, The Great Wine Swindle*) or to inoculate their authors against accusations of such (*Wine for Dummies, The Complete Idiot's Guide to Wine*). The prevailing wisdom seems to be that wine knowledge should be worn lightly and that the most effective means of sharing one's knowledge is to downplay or even poke fun at it.

In the past, this approach made sense and was probably even necessary. There is no denying that wine was a tough sell in America for many decades. Historically, a taste for high culture has often been regarded with suspicion and disdain, an attitude that has extended to habits of the table. Thomas Jefferson, America's first and greatest oenophile, was excoriated by fellow Virginian Patrick Henry for having "abjured his native victuals" in favor of French foods and wines, and for two centuries thereafter, wine was regarded as something Continental, decadent, and elitist. Even after the first shoots of America's wine revolution emerged—the Judgment of Paris in 1976, the arrival of the wine critic Robert Parker a few years later—wine's image problem persisted, and wine writers responded accordingly. The general thrust of the literature was that wine was arcane, intimidating, and exotic and needed to be demystified and spoken of in ways that the man on the street could understand if it was ever going to win over large numbers of Americans.

Some wine writers believe that this is still the case. Eric Asimov, the wine columnist for the *New York Times*, recently wrote a book called *How to Love Wine*, in which he claimed that wine remains horribly intimidating for the layman—that wine experts, with all their jargon and obscure metaphors, create feelings of anxiety and inadequacy in regular people and scare them away from wine. (Asimov, it should be said, writes in a delightfully accessible and genial way and is a source of unfailingly excellent wine advice for his readers.) Asimov contrasted our supposedly cowed wine culture with America's dynamic beer culture: "Beer consumers are a far more confident lot than wine consumers. They're at ease with beer, mostly because they've had a solid grounding in their subject, unlike wine consumers who've been brainwashed into believing they must be educated or taught how to 'appreciate' wine before they can enjoy it." He went on to say that with top-end restaurants starting beer programs and scholarly tomes devoted to beer popping up on bookshelves, "some fear that a consequence will be a rise in the same sort of anxieties and pretentiousness that plague and intimidate wine consumers."

Asimov took some flak for these comments, and not without reason. By beer consumers, he presumably meant beer geeks (beer snobs, if you prefer), as opposed to the muscle-shirt-and-tattoo types swigging Budweiser at the neighborhood tavern. But beer geeks weren't born with that "solid grounding"; they acquired it by tasting, by listening, and by studying. And no one has "brainwashed" wine consumers into thinking that they can't enjoy wine if they don't study it; the point is that one's pleasure can be enhanced by knowing a little something about the subject. Writing in the *Wine Spectator*, the aforementioned Matt Kramer pointedly rebutted Asimov's comments, and it is worth citing his rejoinder in full:

> This is the "cringe." Too many wine lovers are needlessly embarrassed by wine. They feel a need to "democratize" wine

by debasing it. Wine, you see, is too hoity-toity. So it's best if it gets taken down a peg or two. Ironically, nowhere is this more prevalent than among the very intellectuals who have spent a goodly part of their lives becoming educated and are, in turn, educating others. Wine lovers have nothing to apologize for. You don't see music lovers apologizing for suggesting that perhaps you might better understand a concert or even a song if you spend a little time learning about music. You sure as hell don't see art lovers apologizing for the seeming incomprehensibility of so much of contemporary art. If we don't get it, we're unashamedly told, the fault is ours for not bringing enough context to what we're viewing. Whether that's true or not is beside the point. The point is this: Wine, like many other aesthetic pleasures, admits and supports deeper investigation. To suggest that such investigation is worthwhile is hardly "brainwashing" or bullying. It's called education. And that's surely an admirable, worthwhile thing, right?

Yes, it is.

But the bigger problem, it seems to me, is that Asimov was describing a problem that no longer exists. The idea that wine consumers are plagued by "anxieties and pretentiousness" just doesn't accord with the reality of the American wine scene circa the second decade of the twenty-first century. If people are being chased away from wine by all that arcane wine talk, it sure doesn't show up in the data. Indeed, the historic, two-decades-long wine boom that America is experiencing has coincided with the proliferation of Robert Parker–style tasting notes, filled with florid, esoteric descriptions (caramel-coated autumn leaves, anyone?). While it might be a stretch to think that the notes have somehow *encouraged* this budding oenophilia, they clearly have not inhibited it. With more Americans drinking and collecting wine than ever before, it is hard to see exactly how the high-end discourse about wine is serving as a barrier to entry.

The reality is, we live in a very different wine moment now than we did fifteen years ago. I see it all the time—at dinner parties, cocktail receptions, and other social occasions. I meet people who have little, if any, formal wine knowledge but who enjoy drinking wine, are eager to learn more about it, and are not remotely intimidated by it. Even though they know I am a wine writer, they don't hesitate to share their opinions of wines and are not afraid to take issue with mine even though I am supposedly the authority figure (it's the same way with my kids). A few years ago, I hosted a tasting in Chicago at which I served a López de Heredia Rosé. López de Heredia is a great producer of traditional Riojas, but its Rosé is an unorthodox wine; it is aged for a number of years in barrel, and it has a very distinctive oxidative note as a result. It's one of those wines you either like or hate (I'm not sure anyone actually *loves* it), and half the room at the Chicago event hated it and wasn't afraid to let me know. Was I insulted? Hell, no: I found the pushback gratifying. It's a sign of an increasingly confident wine culture.

Like Asimov, I am envious of America's beer culture, but for another reason. With the advent of the craft beer movement, beer has been able to move upmarket, but at no cost to its blue-collar bona fides. The beer geeks and those heavily tattooed Bud drinkers happily coexist. Wine, by contrast, has not been able to bridge the highbrow-lowbrow divide nearly as effortlessly. It is still portrayed in the media and the culture at large as a hobby for rich swells, and every attempt to dumb it down, to make it seem somehow more accessible, ends up just . . . dumbing it down.

(A few years ago, one somewhat prominent wine writer wrote an entire book geared to women in which she compared wines to articles of clothing; she managed both to demean wine and to insult women.) Wine writers, and wine enthusiasts generally, have no need to apologize for their oenophilia and ought to give the apologias a rest. If wine makes some people insecure, that's their problem, not ours. Oenophilia is now just a normal American hobby.

But while we've come a long way as a wine culture, there is one other thing that I would love to see: it would be great if we could get over our fixation on the possible health benefits of wine. In 1991, *60 Minutes* ran a segment calling attention to the so-called French Paradox, which posited that the low rate of heart disease in France, despite a national diet gloriously abundant in foie gras, cheese, and other rich foods, was due to the country's prodigious consumption of red wine. That report led many Americans to start drinking wine, but it also fanned an obsessive interest in the nutritional and therapeutic properties of fermented grape juice, an obsession that endures.

Now, there is no denying that this subject is an interesting one, and it appears that there really is a link between red wine and well-being. It is now widely recognized, for instance, that moderate red wine consumption—generally defined as one or two 5-ounce glasses a day for women and two or three for men, drunk with food—boosts HDL cholesterol, the "good" cholesterol that purges arteries of fatty deposits. In addition, scientists have determined that the flavonoids in red wine have an anticoagulant effect that can help prevent blood clots leading to heart attacks.

Resveratrol, a polyphenol found in grapes, has become a source of particular fascination. It, too, is said to have a role in preventing clots and is believed to inhibit the production of LDL cholesterol, the "bad" kind. Judging by the headlines, resveratrol seems to be the omnipotent ingredient in red wine—a "vascular pipe-cleaner," as one physician put it. Research suggests that resveratrol can delay the aging process and forestall many gerontological diseases, notably Alzheimer's. It is also claimed that this antioxidant can boost stamina, reduce lung inflammation stemming from chronic pulmonary disease, and help stave off cancer and radiation poisoning. Then there is this joyous news, possibly upending age-old assumptions about alcohol and sexual performance: resveratrol apparently works to enhance blood flow, which in turn may improve erectile function.

Personally, I'm thrilled to learn that red wine could help me avoid cancer, outlast opponents on the tennis court, survive a nuclear attack, and lead a long, lucid, and Viagra-free life. However, a little caution is in order. Most of the testing with resveratrol has been done on mice, and they have been given ungodly amounts of the stuff. As the *New York Times* pointed out in a 2006 article, the mice in one experiment were injected with 24 milligrams of resveratrol per kilogram of body weight; red wine contains around 1.5 to 3 milligrams of resveratrol per liter, so to get the equivalent dose, a 150-pound person would need to drink 750 to 1,500 bottles of wine a day. That would be an ambitious undertaking.

Red wine may contain resveratrol, but it contains substantially more alcohol, and regardless of how beneficial wine ultimately proves to be for the heart, lungs, groin, and other body parts, we already know it has a powerful and mostly salutary psychological influence. Wine—or, to be more precise, the alcohol in wine—leaves us happy; it is a relaxant, a stimulant, a balm. It can make a bad day good and a good one better. All this, coupled with the gustatory pleasure that wine confers, ought to be reason enough to uncork a bottle. It is great that science is uncovering so many possible ancillary benefits to red wine, and I hope that resveratrol is indeed the cure-all that mankind has been waiting for. But I think we should just lighten up and enjoy wine for the immediate gratification. Wine is a habit that requires no rationale other than the pursuit of enjoyment.

# 2

⁂

# Becoming a Wine Maven

THREE SIMPLE RULES FOR BECOMING A WINE GEEK

1. Drink often.
2. Drink a wide range of wines.
3. Drink as well as your budget permits.

The last point is particularly important, though I need to tread cautiously here. Nothing brings out the inner Calvinist in some people quite like the prospect of spending more than a few dollars on a bottle of wine. Put a hefty price tag on that Washington State Cabernet Sauvignon and it suddenly seems . . . decadent. The economic travails of recent years have reinforced that parsimony, and even people who had no problem dropping $50 on a bottle of Pinot prior to the Great Recession have scaled back their wine purchases or sharply lowered the price they are willing to pay for a bottle. Everyone is looking for value these days (which is why a later chapter in this book is devoted to value wines), so what I am about to say is a little out of step with the times: generally speaking, the more you are willing to pay, the better you are going to drink, and the better you drink, the more discerning you'll become. To hone an appreciation of wine, you need to taste top-drawer stuff—not every day, not necessarily once a week or even once a month, but often enough to develop a sense of just how good wine can get and what distinguishes the princely stuff from the plonk. No doubt some drinkers will never be able to differentiate a Grand-Puy-Lacoste from a Gallo Hearty Burgundy, but there aren't very many people with palates that leaden; even the completely uninitiated can usually recognize a superior wine when they taste one. And up to a certain point, there is a correlation between price and quality—a $60 *premier cru* Burgundy is going to be a big step up from a $15 Sonoma Pinot Noir. There is a degree of refinement and complexity in a *grand cru* Chablis that you will not find in Yellow Tail Chardonnay, and if you are intent on cultivating your palate, it is good to be familiar with those differences.

## WHAT MAKES FOR A GREAT WINE?

- *Aromatic complexity* A great wine will give off a potpourri of aromas—some sweet (fruit, flowers), others savory (earth, spices)—and will have you dipping your nose in the glass constantly. Some wines literally smell so good that you don't want to taste them.
- *Concentration* A great wine packs a lot of flavor, and those flavors run deep. With some wines you sense a bit of dilution; you'll occasionally hear oenophiles describe a wine as having a "hollow midpalate," which is wine-geek jargon for thinness of flavor. Great wines taste *concentrated*. But note: depth of flavor has nothing to do with depth of color

or density. The lightest, most delicately textured wines can pack huge amounts of flavor.

- *Balance* In a really great wine, the fruit, acidity, and tannins (if it's a red) will be perfectly balanced, and there will be an unmistakable sense of harmony to the wine—a feeling that each element is perfectly integrated and that each is in perfect proportion to the others. Great wines have a seamlessness about them and a sense of completeness—nothing missing, nothing extraneous.

- *Crescendo* I find that truly great wines tend to unfurl slowly in the mouth, building in flavor and intensity as they cross the palate. For me, it is the telltale sign that I've got something special in the glass. Wine geeks refer to this sensation as the "peacock's tail"—the flavors puff up and fan out. Call it what you want, but that peacock's tail or crescendo is another hallmark of a great wine.

- *Length* With a great wine, the flavors persist long after you've swallowed the juice. Sometimes the finish lasts a minute; other times it can linger well beyond that. But persistence is another mark of a brilliant wine.

The most overrated attribute in a wine: fruitiness. Yes, wine is made from grapes, grapes are a fruit, and wine is thus a fruit-based beverage. But the fruitiness in a wine just isn't terribly interesting. Whether it's evocative of cherries, strawberries, or blackberries, it's still just fruit. It smells good, it's part of the pleasure, but I think it is the least compelling aspect of a wine. I'm more drawn to savory elements—herbs, spices, minerality, and so forth. I think the French have it exactly right: the grape, along with the vine, is primarily a vehicle for conveying the influence of the vineyard—the *goût de terroir*, as they put it. The best wines have plenty of ripe, appealing fruit—it is the minimum required—but they offer much more than that: they show aromatics that go far beyond the cherry-and-berry thing, and they exude a real sense of place. A great Châteauneuf-du-Pape, for instance, will have lots of exuberant fruit, but it will give off a strong whiff of lavender and other plants of the *garrigue*, as the fragrant scrub that you find in Provence is known.

The most underrated attribute in a wine: texture. Wine writers use the term *mouth feel* to describe the physical sensation of a wine flowing across the tongue. Alas, the phrase *mouth feel* is a bit clunky; so I prefer to go with *texture*. All wines have texture—some are silky, others chewy, still others borderline syrupy. How we react to a given wine depends in no small part on the tactile sensations we perceive, and that varies from person to person. For instance, I find that I'm almost allergic to Pinot Noirs that display any hints of syrupiness. I want Pinot that's crisp, in which the fruit almost seems crunchy. So much of the discussion about wine focuses on aroma, but the feel of a wine as it moves about the mouth is a hugely important factor in determining whether we like a given bottle.

I won't deny that being a wine writer has its perks, and one of them is that you occasionally get to taste some very special wines. And like many wine obsessives, I not only take detailed notes on those wines, but I add them to a permanent greatest-hits list that I maintain. (Much to my wife's chagrin, I also have a habit of keeping the empty bottles of great wines I've had the pleasure of experiencing; it's a trophy case, you might say.) On the chance that it might interest you—and because we grape nuts are always looking for an opportunity to talk about our conquests—here is my greatest-hits list, and long may it continue to expand:

- 1947 Château Cheval Blanc
- 1996 Domaine J.-F. Coche-Dury Corton Charlemagne
- 1990 Domaine de la Romanée-Conti La Tâche
- 1990 Domaine de la Romanée-Conti Romanée-Conti
- 1971 Domaine de la Romanée-Conti La Tâche
- 1989 Château Haut-Brion
- 1961 Château Haut-Brion
- 1959 Château Haut-Brion
- 1961 Château La Mission Haut-Brion
- 1982 Château Mouton Rothschild
- 1989 Château Pétrus
- 1982 Château Lafleur
- 1988 Krug Champagne Clos du Mesnil
- 1974 Heitz Martha's Vineyard Cabernet Sauvignon
- 1963 Quinta do Noval Vintage Port Nacional
- 1959 Henriot Champagne
- 1991 Domaine Chave Hermitage Cuvée Cathelin
- 1990 Trimbach Riesling Clos Ste. Hune
- 1795 Barbeito Madeira Terrantez

## THE COST OF A WINE EDUCATION

If you are unmarried and free to spend your money however you wish, you can skip this next section. If you are married, engaged, or otherwise in a serious relationship and your partner is not as besotted with wine as you are, you should read it. Wine can cause pain in a relationship—or, to be a bit more exact, spending lots of money on wine can cause problems. That's particularly true if the money is being spent furtively. Take it from me: an incriminating receipt will turn up at some point, and you don't want that (mine was discovered while I was boarding a flight home from Paris; the phone conversation while I was on the tarmac was not an especially cheery one, nor was the face-to-face discussion when I arrived home). One possible solution to this issue is to try to convert your significant other into a fellow wine zealot, but that could wreak havoc on your household finances. It's better just to exercise a little restraint. *Drink as well as your budget permits* doesn't mean busting your budget. It's easy to get carried away, to think that you absolutely must have this or that wine in your cellar. Actually, you don't, and the sooner you realize that, the better off you'll be—and here, too, I'm speaking from experience.

## TASTING NOTES

This may be stating the obvious, but the key to becoming a smarter, more perceptive taster is practice. In his best-selling book *Outliers*, Malcolm Gladwell claimed that to become an expert in any given field requires a minimum of 10,000 hours of practice. I suspect that if a person spent 10,000 hours drinking wine, the result would be a badly pickled brain. Nonetheless, there is no doubt that the best way to become truly knowledgeable about wine and to get to a point where you really know what you are talking about is to sample as many wines as possible. That means drinking a wide array of wines at home and attending as many tastings as you can; wine classes can help, too.

Book knowledge matters greatly in wine as well, and you can learn a lot from reading good books about wine. Five must-have books for the budding wine enthusiast are:

- *Adventures on the Wine Route* Famed importer Kermit Lynch's classic travelogue about viticultural France, full of brilliant insights into French wine culture and the ways and whys of wine.
- *Tasting Pleasures* British wine writer Jancis Robinson's charming, informative memoir about her life as a globe-trotting wine scribe. A book that leaves you excited about wine.
- *Wine for Dummies* Mary Ewing-Mulligan and her husband, Ed McCarthy, did an outstanding job with this book, and it is a great source of basic but indispensable wine knowledge.
- *Bordeaux* Robert Parker's comprehensive guide to the wines of Bordeaux. Packed with useful information, but the real value of the book is in showing how to think analytically about what's in the glass. Even if you don't share Parker's taste, you can learn from him.
- *Matt Kramer on Wine* Kramer is arguably America's finest wine commentator, and this greatest-hits collection of his columns is delicious food for thought about all aspects of wine and wine culture.

The ultimate learning tool is tasting, but it is not enough just to taste wines; you also need to take notes on them. Tasting notes are a controversial topic in the wine world. The argument against them is that in addition to all the outlandish descriptors—*sweaty saddle, beef blood, pencil shavings, cat piss, wet dog*—they offer a cramped, reductive vision of what wine is all about. They also portray wine as a static, unchanging product, when in fact the best wines often evolve dramatically in the bottle and the glass.

How to put wine into words is a subject that tortures wine

writers like no other. True, wine tasting is not the only gustatory experience that is difficult to convey linguistically; it is certainly not easy to describe how a steak tastes or to capture the flavor of an oyster in a few pithy comments. But for restaurant critics, at least, the descriptive imperatives are generally less onerous: they are not obligated to describe each dish in exquisite, multisentence detail, and they can pad their reviews with lots of scene-setting. Not so wine critics: they are expected to talk only about what's in the bottle and to construct what amounts to a three-dimensional view of a Cabernet or Chardonnay—and words rarely seem adequate to the task.

In 1978, Robert Parker began publishing *The Wine Advocate*, and although Parker uses his share of slippery adjectives (*hedonistic, sexy, intellectual*), his tasting notes have always stood out for their no-nonsense, just-the-flavors-ma'am approach. Here's Parker, for instance, on the 1996 vintage of Château d'Yquem, the great sweet wine of Bordeaux: "Light gold with a tight but promising nose of roasted hazelnuts intermixed with crème brûlée, vanilla beans, honey, orange marmalade, and peach."

Thanks to Parker's influence, this kind of tasting note has become the industry standard over the past quarter century or so; most critics nowadays make a point of listing the aromas, flavors, and tactile sensations they perceive in a wine. These grab bags of descriptors can breed a certain awe and deference among many wine enthusiasts (*Gee, this guy must really be talented if he can smell kaffir lime and poached Anjou pear in this wine—I should take his advice!*), which is undoubtedly part of the reason wine writers like to use them. But as you would imagine, the cherry-and-berry metaphors, not to mention more offbeat comparisons, have also drawn a lot of criticism and ridicule. When it comes to tasting notes, the line between incisive and overwrought can be a fine one. The British wine expert Michael Broadbent once likened a wine's bouquet to the smell of schoolgirls' uniforms (no, he wasn't arrested). And the late Auberon (son of Evelyn) Waugh, in his wine column for Britain's *Tatler*, described one wine as smelling of "a dead chrysanthemum on the grave of a stillborn West Indian baby" (no, he wasn't fired, but he and his editor, Tina Brown, were taken before the Press Council to answer charges of insensitivity).

Who can blame people for yukking it up? "Professional" tasting notes are filled with lots of comically obscure references and ridiculous metaphors like these. (I put "professional" in quotation marks because the use of that word could be taken to suggest that wine critics are pros who possess superior tasting skills. But while some critics are indeed good tasters, others are not, and because wine writing is a self-selecting field with few barriers to entry, I am not a fan of using the word *professional* to describe wine writers. Forgive the digression.) But many of the aromas and flavors often cited in tasting notes actually do have a chemical basis—we're not entirely bluffing. Some of the most commonly observed aromas in wines—toast, butter, vanilla, citrus, apples, cherries, pears, honey, herbs—are there because of volatile organic compounds that either were in the grapes themselves or seeped into the finished juice. For instance, the buttery note often found in Chardonnays is an aroma compound called diacetyl, which is a by-product of malolactic fermentation (a secondary fermentation that softens the acidity in wines). I see no reason that wine writers or wine enthusiasts should shy away from noting these aromas if they detect them, and when it comes to flaws such as volatile acidity (which smells like vinegar or nail polish remover) and brettanomyces (which gives wines a barnyard aroma), they absolutely should call them out.

I think the biggest problem with contemporary tasting notes

is that the effort to sniff out all sorts of aromas seems to have become an end in itself for many oenophiles. The point of a tasting note is to tell the story of a wine with brevity, clarity, and, hopefully, a little brio, and to give it a thumbs-up or -down. I'm a lot less interested in learning the exact species of cherry that someone detects in a red Burgundy than in finding out whether the wine is good or bad, what's good or bad about it, and when might be the best time to drink it. Also, because wines evolve both in the glass and in the bottle, the aromatics can change quickly; the nose is just taking a snapshot, which is another reason not to get too carried away with the descriptors.

All that said, as part of the self-education process, I think it is worth taking tasting notes. The act of jotting down your impressions of wines necessarily concentrates the mind—it obliges you to be a more attentive taster, and a more attentive taster is usually a better taster and derives more satisfaction from wines. You may not need 10,000 hours of practice to become a more knowledgeable and perceptive judge of wines, but you do need to bring a certain rigor to the effort, and writing tasting notes serves that function; it makes you think more analytically than might otherwise be the case.

So what exactly should you be writing down in your tasting notes? To begin with, I think it is worth noting the color of a wine: How deep a shade of red or yellow is it? Does it look young or old? Obviously you need to smell the wine; what aromas do you detect? Don't drive yourself nuts trying to determine whether it's raspberries or strawberries that you smell; it is enough just to say *red berries*, or even just *red fruits*. How does the wine taste—is the fruit crisp and fresh, or is it kind of jammy? What is the texture like? As you run the wine around your mouth, do you pick up the acidity? Does the wine seem balanced, harmonious, or does it taste a little disjointed? After you swallow, do the flavors linger for a long time, or does the aftertaste quickly fade? And what about the tannins, which cause that astringent feeling after you swallow a red wine—do they seem like they are nicely integrated, or do they stick out a bit? These are the things you want to note while recording your overall feelings about the wine. And don't be afraid to compare your impressions with those of professional critics. This, too, is part of the learning process. However flawed "professional" tasting notes might be, useful information can be gleaned from them regarding the particulars of individual wines and in terms of how to think about wine more generally.

A word of warning: writing tasting notes in the company of non–wine geeks may invite some ridicule. Be strong and ignore it. A word of advice: write your notes electronically, or if you plan to do it by hand (so last century), be sure to get a dedicated notebook. Don't make the mistake of writing down your notes on random scraps of paper (and here I also speak from experience); it's too easy to lose those scraps, and even if you don't lose them, they'll end up as a disorganized pile of paper, which won't do you much good.

## THE EVOLUTION OF A WINE GEEK

We all have to start somewhere, and for most American wine enthusiasts, that somewhere is California. The United States is the home market for California wines, and it stands to reason that these tend to be the gateway wines for American drinkers. Lots of people never move beyond California; they are perfectly content drinking only Napa Cabernets and Sonoma Chardonnays. Simplicity has its virtues, and there's no shame in sticking with what you like. But the wine world is a big, fabulously diverse place, and arguably the greatest pleasure that oenophilia offers is the pleasure of discovery—of finding new grapes, regions, and wines. Brillat-Savarin said that "the discovery of a new dish does more for human happiness than the discovery of a new star." The same can be said of discovering new wines—it not only excites the palate, it serves to reaffirm one's passion for fermented grape juice.

In terms of changing tastes and expanded horizons, it is interesting to note that the traffic all seems to flow in one direction: New World to Old. Rarely, if ever, do you see Burgundy fans or Bordeaux diehards shifting their allegiances to the New World. By contrast, it is commonplace for oenophiles reared on New World wines to experience Damascene conversions, suddenly swearing off California or Australian wines with the same fervor that they once embraced them and filling up their cellars with Barolos and Bandols. Why the one-way flow of traffic? Speaking very broadly, I think that as people get deeper into wine, they place greater value on subtlety and complexity, and in general, Old World wines deliver more of both. I suspect another factor is romance. To be blunt, there is just not a lot of it in New World wine regions, whereas European viticulture is dominated by small, artisanal producers. Napa is beautiful, but it simply doesn't exude the kind of charm you find in, say, the Loire or Alsace. And romance is unquestionably a big selling point for wines, for wineries, and for wine regions.

So how does wine's evolutionary process unfold? For American wine enthusiasts, it usually goes something like this: They start out drinking Napa Cabernets, perhaps with some Australian reds thrown in. Then they find some Old World wine that wows them—maybe a Bordeaux or a Châteauneuf-du-Pape (Americans, reared on big California reds, seem to have a particular fondness for Châteauneuf-du-Papes, the ultimate Big French

Reds). Having thus crossed the Atlantic, metaphorically speaking, they make new discoveries—Côte-Rôties, Chiantis, Riojas. Maybe they lose all interest in New World wines; maybe they start buying Old and New World wines. We Burgundy fans like to say that all roads lead to Burgundy, and it is true that many oenophiles do eventually succumb to Burgundy's siren lure. A lot of wine drinkers are finding their way to Burgundy faster than ever these days. For one thing, Burgundy is very fashionable right now with sommeliers and writers, which is naturally sparking heightened consumer interest in the wines. Also, Pinot Noir has become hugely popular in the past decade, and while a lot of people start out drinking California, Oregon, or New Zealand Pinots, curiosity or serendipity eventually leads them to Pinot's heartland, Burgundy.

You often hear wine buffs say, "I've got an Old World palate" or "I've got a New World palate." What they are saying is that their preferences lean heavily in one direction or the other. One has to be careful about generalizing when it comes to wine— there are always significant exceptions to the rule—and the dividing line between Old World and New World has been blurring over the past fifteen years. Climate change and stylistic shifts have been bumping up the alcohol levels in Europe; in the 2009 vintage, for instance, some Bordeaux weighed in at well over 14 percent alcohol. Meanwhile, a growing number of New World winemakers, especially in California, are moving away from the fruit-forward, high-alcohol style; they are seeking out cooler sites that can produce leaner, earthier wines. All that said, the New World/Old World dichotomy is still a valid one. Most New World wines continue to show a very different flavor profile from that of European wines. They tend to be more exuberantly fruity, with higher alcohol contents (14 or 15 percent is normal in California) and rounder, softer textures. People accustomed to this style, when first experiencing a leaner, more acidic Burgundy or Barolo, might well find themselves offering a variation on that old W. C. Fields line: Who took the wine out of my wine? But again, judging by the traffic flow, the Old World style has no difficulty winning new fans.

If you are not sure which side of the divide you belong on, or if you want to put your declared preferences to the test, here's a suggestion: gather up a bunch of Old World and New World wines, put the bottles in paper bags, and taste them blind with some family or friends. They should be similar wines—say, New Zealand Pinot Noirs versus red Burgundies, or white Burgundies versus California Chardonnays. It is fun and can be very revealing.

## WINE TOOLS

Like most hobbies, wine offers lots of accessories that are meant to enhance your drinking pleasure. Wine storage units, grape-specific glasses, splashy decanters, fancy corkscrews—without much effort, an oenophile can blow a fortune on wine gear, and plenty of merchants are more than happy to help you do so. But how many wine gizmos do you really need, and how much should you spend on them? The answer depends in part on how seriously you take the wine thing. If you are buying reasonably expensive bottles, you do need a good place to store them. If you have a basement that's dark, relatively humid, and consistently cool—say, 55 to 60 degrees—you can park all your collectible wines there and they will mature beautifully. If you don't have a space that meets these requirements, a temperature-controlled wine cabinet would be a wise investment. Good storage matters a lot.

Good stemware matters, too, a point that the irrepressible Riedel family has driven home with remarkable success over the years. An Austrian glassmaking dynasty, the Riedels have made themselves virtually synonymous with high-quality wine stemware, and they produce a dizzying array of glasses (decanters, too). There is a Chianti glass, a Montrachet glass, a Grüner Veltliner glass—there's a specific Riedel glass for every major grape variety (and some not-so-major) and virtually every major wine region. The Riedels contend that their glasses are designed to show each particular wine in the most flattering light, and I'm sure that's true. But do you really need an Oregon Pinot Noir glass or a Brunello di Montalcino stem? With all due respect to the Riedels, I'd say no. When it comes to the question of stemware, I've become a fanatical minimalist. In fact, I've whittled myself down to just two types of glasses, Bordeaux stems and Burgundy stems. The latter I use exclusively for red Burgundies and other Pinot Noirs, and everything else goes in a Bordeaux glass, including white wines and sparkling wines. (Champagne flutes are nice to look at and hold, but a wider glass does a better job of bringing out the aromatics; I've noticed that Champagne producers almost never use Champagne flutes during tastings.) I also don't use Riedel glasses, because they can shatter easily and are really expensive. Instead I use Spiegelau glasses; it is a line of stemware that is owned by the Riedels, and it offers excellent glasses that are quite inexpensive—$7 or $8 per stem, which is cheap enough to break.

With regard to that other indispensable tool, the corkscrew, my advice is similar: the $3 variety available at your local package store is all you really need. Yes, there are much more elaborate corkscrews on the market, but unless you are regularly opening eighty-year-old wines, why bother? The simple waiter's corkscrew, as it is known, will do just fine. Unless money is no object, don't go crazy with wine accessories. Buy only what you really need, keep it inexpensive, and spend any extra money on wine.

## YOU'RE THE WINE GUY—YOU PICK THE WINE

It is normally the case that when a group that includes a wine enthusiast goes out to a restaurant, the wine guy will be asked to order the wines—and in truth most oenophiles want and expect to be handed the wine list (though it's best if they are polite and refrain from just grabbing it). But once the list is in hand, it can be a real burden, and not just because it might weigh a lot. If the wine guy isn't picking up the tab for the table, choosing the wines can be tricky. It's especially challenging if the oenophile is a guest. The desire to drink something compelling must be weighed against budgetary considerations and the need to be tactful. Sadly, being given the wine list does not usually give you carte blanche to order whatever you wish, and there is nothing that can spoil a good evening quite like an unexpected $1,500 wine bill. So how to negotiate this delicate matter? Matt Kramer of the *Wine Spectator* has what I think is a smart solution: he looks for inexpensive off-beat wines, pleasant obscurities that the rest of the table will probably be unfamiliar with, that might win a convert or two, and that won't cause any fainting spells when the check arrives.

## WHAT'S A GOOD PALATE, AND HOW DO YOU KNOW IF YOU HAVE ONE?

Spend an evening with a group of wine obsessives and there's an excellent chance that at some point you will hear them assessing the strengths and weaknesses of other people's palates. It could be a major critic, a friend, a colleague, a family member. *Palate* is wine-geek shorthand for tasting chops—for the quality of one's judgments about wine. The ultimate tribute that can be paid an oenophile is to have it be said that he or she possesses a "great palate." It is like telling an art enthusiast that he has an unerring eye or a music buff that she has a flawless ear.

But wait—isn't wine appreciation a completely subjective exercise, and if so, who's to say that someone has a superior or inferior palate? That's a good question, and the short, glib answer is that a good palate is one that you happen to agree with. The reality is that wine appreciation is to a large extent subjective. I'm stating the acutely obvious here, but taste is personal, determined both by one's biological attributes and by things such as experience, expectation, and culture, intangibles that obviously vary from individual to individual. You might love a robust, heady Australian Shiraz, while the same wine might strike me as a hot, syrupy mess. If I tasted the wine on your recommendation, I'd probably think less of your palate, and if I told you what I really thought of the wine, you'd probably think less of mine. Neither of us would necessarily be right or wrong; the difference of opinion would be at least partly rooted in personal taste, in factors beyond our control.

But wine appreciation is not wholly subjective. The British philosopher Barry C. Smith points out that wines have objective qualities that exist independent of our ability to discern them, and he boldly contends that "good tasters are those who get matters right . . . There are standards by which we can judge a wine, or musical score, or painting to be better than another, and these reflect discernible properties of those objects, though it may take practice and experience to recognize them." Interestingly, researchers have found that in experienced tasters, such as sommeliers, more areas of the brain are activated when tasting than is the case in novices, which suggests that experience promotes greater discernment. The fact that major critics seem to agree about individual wines far more often than they disagree likewise suggests that qualitative differences between wines are at least partially rooted in objective properties—that quality isn't just a matter of personal taste.

Of those objective properties, the most important ones to be able to recognize are flaws. At the very least, you need to be able to tell when a wine is damaged (one thing that never fails to amaze me is how often I have seen wine journalists, some quite prominent, flunk this basic test). Easily the most common problem is cork taint, which affects anywhere from 5 to 10 percent of wines bottled under natural cork. If a wine smells like damp cardboard and tastes as if its flavors have been leached out, it is a corked bottle and should be returned to the store (assuming it was bought fairly recently; if it is a thirty-year-old wine, you are probably out of luck). If a wine smells like a particularly pungent barnyard or like vinegar, it is also an off bottle. There are also visual cues you should look for. If the cork on a relatively young bottle is soaked through with wine, or if the cork has clearly moved, the bottle has suffered heat damage and should be returned. If a young white wine shows a surprisingly deep, mature color and smells like Sherry, it has suffered oxidation and should be returned to the store or tossed. If a fairly young red wine looks oddly mature in color, it has probably suffered the same fate. It won't hurt you to drink wines with any of these defects; you just won't be drinking particularly pleasurable wines.

And who are these people referred to as *supertasters*, and are they really superior tasters? The term *supertaster* was coined in 1991 by Linda Bartoshuk, a professor of otolaryngology and psychology at the Yale School of Medicine. Some sixty years earlier, Arthur L. Fox, a scientist for DuPont, had discovered that the chemical compound phenylthiocarbamide, or PTC, tasted oppressively bitter to some people but elicited no response in others; the former were dubbed tasters, the latter nontasters, and the differences were put down to genetic variation. In the 1970s, concerns about the toxicity of PTC led Bartoshuk and other scientists to begin using propylthiouracil, or PROP, instead to test for sensitivity to bitterness. During the course of her research, Bartoshuk noticed that not all tasters reacted the same way to PROP; all of them found it bitter, but a minority found it excruciatingly so. Intrigued, she began studying the tongue anatomy of these individuals and found that they tended to have much denser concentrations of fungiform papillae, the structures at the end of the tongue that house our taste buds. Nor were they sensitive only to bitterness; they seemed to experience much more heightened taste sensations in general. Bartoshuk and her Yale colleagues dubbed these individuals supertasters, a name that clearly implied that they possessed not just sensitive palates but superior ones.

But that just ain't so. The term *supertaster* is really a misnomer —there is no evidence that these individuals are better tasters. In fact, when it comes to wine, being a supertaster is probably more of a liability than anything else. To begin with, supertasters do not particularly enjoy the flavor of alcohol and often complain that it leaves a burning sensation in their mouths. They are also sensitive to astringency and acidity, which can be equally problematic as wine goes. In his book *The Science of Wine*, the British wine writer Jamie Goode highlighted the work of Gary Pickering, a professor of oenology at Canada's Brock University. Pickering had been investigating the relationship between PROP sensitivity and wine appreciation and believed that being a super-taster was no blessing. "I would speculate that supertasters probably enjoy wine less than the rest of us," Pickering told Goode. "They experience astringency, acidity, bitterness, and heat (from alcohol) more intensely, and this combination may make wine—or some wine styles—relatively unappealing."

However, even engaging in this kind of speculation gives the supertaster idea more weight than it deserves. When it comes to understanding sensory perception, we are literally at the tip of the tongue. We know that fungiform papillae are a reliable indicator of sensitivity to the five basic taste sensations; people with very dense concentrations of these structures are more sensitive to bitter, sour, sweet, salty, and savory (umami) flavors than people with average or subaverage concentrations. But while fungiform papillae have been studied exhaustively, much less is known about the papillae on the side of the tongue (foliate papillae) and those toward the back of it (circumvallate papillae), except that we know they also affect how tastes and textures are perceived.

As for the genetic dimension, TAS2R38, the gene associated with being a supertaster, is one of thirty-five bitter receptor genes that have been identified thus far; there may be others. There appears to be little, if any, correlation between PROP/PTC sensitivity and sensitivity to other bitter compounds. Whether the TAS2R38 genotype is indicative of overall taste sensitivity has generated considerable debate; it might be, and it might not be. Most people who show extreme sensitivity to PROP have the two dominant alleles for TAS2R38, but that is not true in all cases. Meanwhile, scientists have identified receptors for sweetness and umami but have no idea which chemical stimuli, like PROP and PTC with bitterness, can reliably test these receptors. Sourness and saltiness are largely uncharted territory. For all these reasons, and also because the concept has been so often misunderstood and misrepresented in the media, many geneticists are reluctant even to use the term *supertaster*.

Beyond all this, we know that the nose wields much more influence over our flavor perceptions than the tongue. And beyond all *that*, we know that our gustatory preferences are determined by a wide variety of factors, most of which have nothing to do with our physiological attributes. The key distinction here is between perceptions and preferences. We may be hardwired to receive flavor stimuli in a certain way, but that information is immediately relayed to the brain, where it is processed through a variety of filters unrelated to our biological dispositions. Our preferences are formed mostly by experience, expectations, culture, and other intangibles.

## 3

---

# How to Buy Wine

HERE ARE few things that get oenophiles more jazzed than finding a seriously good wine shop, with an extensive, interesting selection and a passionate staff. An attractively designed, well-curated brick-and-mortar wine shop is bliss—a place to taste, to buy, and otherwise to indulge one's wine fanaticism. Although wine shops are nothing if not ubiquitous, really good ones are rare. The vast majority of stores have uninspired selections and personnel to match. And even shops with commendable offerings often lack spirited salesmanship. One of the biggest, and I think more unfortunate, stories of the past twenty-five years has been the effect that "professional" wine ratings have had on the retail sector. Many stores stopped selling wine and essentially just started selling scores given by Robert Parker and the *Wine Spectator*. Many people contend that these ratings are more reliable than anything merchants might have to say—that merchants can't be trusted to give good advice because they are chiefly interested in making the sale. I've never quite understood this argument. To begin with, a good retailer will not fill his store with wines that he doesn't like; if he tells you a wine is terrific, it's usually because he really feels that way. Also, most retailers depend on repeat business; foisting bad wines on customers is therefore not a particularly shrewd strategy. In any case, ratings and shelf talkers have become a crutch for the retail sector, and too many stores have taken the easy way out and relied on Parker and *Spectator* points to make the sales for them.

But that is changing now, and I think a golden age of wine retailing may be on the horizon. For one thing, fewer and fewer wine enthusiasts are paying attention to the critics. They know what they like, or they are getting recommendations from other sources, or they no longer regard Parker and the *Spectator* as particularly reliable. Whatever the reason or combination of reasons, ratings seem to matter a lot less than they did a decade ago. Also, competition is forcing smaller retailers to up their game. Big-box stores, supermarkets, and even drugstores are peddling wine these days, and while they sell a lot of plonk, they also sell some good wines. To survive, small retailers increasingly need to differentiate themselves, and creating a store with a well-defined point of view and an enthusiastic, knowledgeable staff is not only a smart survival strategy; in some markets, it may be the *only* survival strategy. A lot of really interesting wine stores are popping up in cities across America, and I expect that trend to continue.

Of course, that doesn't necessarily mean you can buy from them. To regulate liquor sales more effectively after Prohibition was repealed in 1933, most states put in place laws requiring an intermediary, the wholesaler, between the producer of an alcoholic beverage and the retailer. These regulations were enacted at a time when the U.S. wine industry was moribund and few Americans had an interest in wine. It is a very different story now: the country has several thousand wineries and millions of wine enthusiasts, and with the advent of online shopping and the ease and affordability of long-distance shipping, the three-tier distribution system has become an absurdly outdated barrier to free trade and consumer choice. Most states now permit some form of direct-to-consumer shipping from wineries, but the wholesalers are a well-financed interest group and have used their political muscle to limit the scope of many direct-shipping bills and to keep the existing regulatory framework intact. And direct-to-consumer shipping from wineries is just one part of this battle. At present, only around a dozen states allow people to have wine shipped to them from out-of-state retailers. The direct shipping issue is a sad commentary on the state of American politics—for one thing, it underscores how irredeemably corrupt our campaign finance system is—and a source of endless frustration to wine enthusiasts.

These archaic laws have inhibited the growth of online wine buying, but there is still something to be said for the pleasure of browsing and buying in an actual store as opposed to a virtual one. When you're in a brick-and-mortar store, however, there is something you need to check the moment you set foot inside, before you even peruse the selection: Is the temperature relatively cool, or is the heat blasting? If the store is noticeably warm, you should perform an immediate about-face and leave. It doesn't matter how good the inventory is if the wines are not properly stored. I don't care if you see a bottle of 1945 Mouton Rothschild being offered for $200—if the shop is warm, head for the door (and if they're selling '45 Mouton at that price, it's probably a counterfeit bottle anyway). A cellar should be kept at around 55 degrees Fahrenheit, and while a store doesn't need to be quite that cold, it certainly needs to be on the cooler side, and the bottles should be cool to the touch. One other piece of advice: as the saying goes, it pays to shop around, at least to the extent that you can, given our onerous shipping laws. There are sometimes significant price discrepancies between one store and the next, and you can save yourself a few dollars here and there by comparing prices. The best way to do that: use Wine-Searcher.com. It is a great service and can help you find bargains or at least avoid forking over more money than you need to spend.

## SHOULD YOU USE "PROFESSIONAL" WINE RATINGS?

I don't agree with people who contend that all rating scales are irredeemably flawed or who believe that comparative evaluations are somehow antithetical to the culture of wine. Since the beginning of wine, people have been making comparative assessments: I like wine X more than I like wine Y. The 1855 rankings in Bordeaux and the classification system in Burgundy are rooted in such judgments. It is human nature to compare and contrast, and frankly, it is part of the pleasure of wine. I think ratings are an inevitable aspect of wine appreciation, and I certainly haven't been able to resist the urge to keep score; I use letter grades instead of numbers, but it still amounts to scorekeeping.

However, the 100-point scale, popularized by Parker and used by the *Wine Spectator* and other publications, is a farce. It gives a pseudo-objective gloss to what is an almost wholly subjective exercise. I think that unless a critic can, tasting blind, reproduce the same results over and over, he or she has no business assigning a specific score to a wine—and I'm reasonably certain no one can do that. Wines show sufficient variability from bottle to bottle, and the human palate is sufficiently fickle, that that kind of consistency is just not possible. Some years ago, David Shaw of the *Los Angeles Times*, in an otherwise adulatory profile of

Parker, tried to test the famed critic's consistency by having him blind-taste and score a group of wines twice over consecutive days. Parker wouldn't do it, telling Shaw, "I've got everything to lose and nothing to gain." Give him 100 points for candor. In an interview with a Florida newspaper in 2007, Parker made another surprisingly frank admission that ought to have been the death knell of the 100-point scale. "I really think probably the only difference between a 96-, 97-, 98-, 99-, and 100-point wine," he said, "is really the emotion of the moment."

That comment didn't sink the 100-point approach, but the scale may be dying now for another reason: grade inflation. Nowadays critics have powerful incentives to bump up their scores. High scores are catnip for retailers, who use them to flog wines via shelf talkers and e-mail offers. In turn, those citations are excellent free publicity for critics. In a crowded marketplace for wine information, big numbers can help a critic to stand out, and I don't think there is any doubt that score inflation has become rampant. Just look at Parker himself: for the 2010 and 2009 vintages in the northern Rhône Valley of France, he gave out seventeen 100-point ratings. This came not long after he awarded nineteen 100-point ratings to the 2009 vintage in Bordeaux and eighteen 100-point scores during a retrospective tasting of the 2002 Napa vintage. In a ten-month span, Parker gave out fifty-three 100-point ratings. Who knew perfection was so pervasive? When every wine these days seems to get 90 points just for showing up and scores in the mid- and high 90s are given out like candy on Halloween, it is hard to assign much credibility to ratings—and it appears that fewer and fewer consumers and merchants are taking them seriously (a growing number of wine stores nationwide are now point-free zones).

Does that mean you should never trust ratings? No. If you

can find a critic whose taste in wine more or less aligns with yours, then by all means use his or her scores. If two or three critics agree that a particular wine is brilliant, there's probably some wisdom in that crowd. But just recognize that grade inflation is everywhere these days, and just because Parker or the *Spectator* gushes about a wine, that doesn't necessarily mean that you are going to gush about it. Caveat emptor, as they say.

## VINTAGE: DOES IT MATTER?

If you carry around a vintage chart in your wallet, here's a suggestion: throw it out. For one thing, vintage summaries are easily found on smartphones and tablets, so there's no need to keep cluttering up your wallet. More importantly, vintage charts are now meaningless. It used to be that there were good vintages and bad ones. These days, it seems, there are only good vintages and better ones. Thanks to improvements in winemaking and warmer, more consistent growing seasons, it now takes something truly cataclysmic—think biblical, think locusts and frogs—to ruin an entire harvest. Short of that, almost no vintage is without good wines. Yet as the qualitative differences between vintages have narrowed, the buzz over certain vintages has grown cacophonous. This seems to be a particularly American phenomenon. While Americans are arguably the savviest wine drinkers on the planet these days, we do have a tendency to fall prey to the Bright Shiny Object Syndrome—to swoon over extravagantly hyped vintages and to shun those that are not as highly touted.

Sure, some extraordinary vintages deserve the hype they generate. In 2005, Bordeaux and Burgundy both produced incredible wines, two of the finest vintages that these regions have ever had. The most acclaimed wines were amazingly good, and not surprisingly, they were staggeringly expensive. (Case in point: in the early 2000s, I was able to buy Domaine Mugnier's Musigny, a fabulous *grand cru* red Burgundy, for around $80 a bottle in France; when the 2005 Mugnier Musigny was released, its price instantly soared to $5,000 a bottle. Needless to say, I'm no longer a buyer of Monsieur Mugnier's Musigny.) But 2005 yielded great wines at all price points, and fabulous Burgundies and Bordeaux were to be had for $25 and $30 a bottle. In the case of the 2005 vintage, it paid to believe the hype.

But not all highly touted vintages merit the acclaim. For instance, the *Wine Spectator* gave the 2000 vintage in Italy's Piedmont region a 100-point rating. But among Barolo and Barbaresco producers and collectors, the *Spectator*'s rating was considered a bit of a joke. Yes, some excellent wines were produced in 2000, but it was widely agreed that 1996 and 2001 were much stronger vintages (and the *Spectator* has since downgraded the 2000 Piedmont vintage, now rating it 93 points). Just as critics have lots of incentive to give out high scores for individual wines, they also have incentive to hype every promising vintage that comes along, and that's because buzz sells. But the hype isn't always justified. How do you find out when it is and when it isn't? That's tough. A trusted retailer can help. Following the chatter on a wine discussion board such as wineberserkers.com can also help. But the most reliable way of determining whether a vintage is overhyped or appropriately hyped is simply to taste some of the wines yourself.

Here's something else to keep in mind. All the buzz over vintage obscures an essential point: the producer matters more than the vintage, and great producers make excellent wines pretty much every year. Even under the most favorable conditions, a middling producer is not likely to make a brilliant wine. By contrast, a gifted vintner can turn out compelling wines even under the most challenging conditions—and it is often those wines that they are most proud of. If you were a producer in Burgundy who failed to make a fabulous wine in 2005, when the conditions could not have been more favorable, you should probably be in another line of work. In contrast, 2008 was a very challenging year, with lots of rain and rot in the vineyards, but the finest producers in Burgundy still managed to craft excellent wines—not as strong as their '05s, to be sure, but delicious wines in their own right, and much more attractively priced. The point is this: don't let yourself succumb to the Bright Shiny Object Syndrome. Some intelligent buying in so-called off years can yield a lot of drinking pleasure.

## BUYING FOREIGN WINES

Obviously, imported wines can be intimidating ones to buy. The names are unfamiliar, and the bottles often don't list the grape or grapes used to make the wine. By law, for instance, most French wines are labeled according to their place of origin, not the grape or grapes that went into the bottle. (The major exception is in the Alsace region, where the wines are identified by the grape.) Chablis, for instance, is a region in northern France, not far from Paris; the wines we know as Chablis come from this region and are made from the Chardonnay grape, but producers are not allowed to put the word *Chardonnay* on their labels. This stricture is rooted in the notion of *terroir*, which is the cornerstone of French viticulture—the belief that the vineyard is the most important component in the winemaking process and that the grape is merely a vehicle for conveying the voice of the soil, the *terroir*. Most Italian and Spanish wines are also labeled by place rather than grape.

## WHAT'S IN A NAME?

Should the French ease up and allow producers to put grape names on their bottles? It's a contentious issue. France's winemaking tradition is rooted in the notion that the vineyard matters more than the grape and that a wine's first duty is to express a sense of place; allowing winemakers in Burgundy, Bordeaux, and Rhône to label their wines by grape variety rather than site would be a repudiation of that centuries-old heritage and the philosophy that has guided it. But it's also the case that millions of consumers around the world buy their wines according to the grape name, and lots of them don't drink French wines in part because the labels confound them. They go to the store looking for a Chardonnay, see a French wine labeled Mâcon-Lugny, and don't realize that a Mâcon-Lugny *is* a Chardonnay (and the kid working behind the counter might not know it, either). For the collector crowd, there is no such confusion, and there is no need to list the grape varieties on, say, a bottle of Château Haut-Brion. At the discount end of the global wine market, however, the French have seen a huge loss of business over the past fifteen years, and their competitive position would probably be helped by allowing lower-priced wines to be sold by grape names.

But even though imported wines can be intimidating, there is actually an easy, almost fail-safe way to find good ones: flip the bottle around and see who imported it. Importers have played a central, even defining role in the emergence and growth of American wine culture. Combining impeccable taste with evangelical zeal, people such as Kermit Lynch, Robert Chadderdon, Robert Haas, and Terry Theise have not only introduced Americans to many of the greatest wines that Europe has to offer; they have also helped cultivate several generations of palates. But the wine world has broadened dramatically in the decades since these importers started out; entire regions—entire countries—that produced mostly rotgut twenty years ago are now making respectable wines. Amid this global quality revolution, a number of newer importers are continuing the work started by Lynch, Chadderdon, and their generation and are scouring the Languedoc, Galicia, Sicily, Mendoza, and McLaren Vale for tomorrow's star winemakers.

Here is a list of importers whose wines can be counted on to deliver pleasure:

AUSTRALIA
> Epicurean Wines
> Old Bridge Cellars
> The Australian Premium Wine Collection

AUSTRIA
> Winemonger
> Monika Caha Selections

FRANCE
> Kermit Lynch Wine Merchant
> Alain Junguenet/Wines of France
> Becky Wasserman Selections
> Robert Kacher Selections
> Dan Kravitz/Hand Picked Selections
> Jenny & François Selections

Jon-David Headrick Selections
Roy Cloud/Vintage '59 Imports
Martine's Wines

FRANCE/GERMANY/AUSTRIA
Savio Soares Selections

FRANCE/ITALY
Rosenthal Wine Merchant

FRANCE/ITALY/SPAIN/GERMANY
Louis/Dressner Selections

GERMANY
Rudi Wiest Selections

GERMANY/AUSTRIA/CHAMPAGNE
Terry Theise Estate Selections

ITALY
Marc de Grazia Selections
Leonardo LoCascio/Winebow
Neil Empson Selections
Vias Imports
Domaine Select Wine Estates

SPAIN
José Pastor Selections
De Maison Selections
Gerry Dawes Selections—the Spanish Artisan Wine Group
Jorge Ordóñez

Olé Imports
Grapes of Spain

SPAIN/FRANCE
Eric Solomon/European Cellars

EVERYWHERE
Michael Skurnik Wines
Polaner Selections
Vineyard Brands
Kysela Père et Fils
Weygandt-Metzler

## COLLECTING WINE

People collect wines for two reasons: so they can drink them at a later date and so they can sell them for a profit at a later date. Wine investing can take different forms. Collectors will sometimes buy two cases of a wine, intending to sell one of them for a tidy profit so they can drink the other one effectively for free. But some people buy wine purely for investment purposes; in fact, some wine investment funds are now available to "high net worth" individuals, as they are known. (Wine is what's referred to by financial wizards as an "alternative asset class." Nothing like Wall Street jargon to drain the romance out of something.) These funds invest in blue-chip wines—mostly top-growth Bordeaux—and pay out investors in cash; the wines are never actually consumed. It is no surprise that people have started wine investment funds: over the past thirty years, wines such as the 1982 Château Pétrus have delivered amazing returns. However, those huge returns are probably a thing of the past, and wine speculation, if not exactly immoral, is certainly antithetical to what wine is all about.

If people wish to buy Pétrus purely for investment purposes, that's certainly their prerogative—and I have the right to belittle the practice. Sure, wine is a business. But it is also a beverage, meant to be drunk. Hemingway once said that wine is "the most civilized thing in the world," and he was right. To reduce wine to a mere commodity, to see it as no different from pork bellies or gold bars, strikes me as completely counter to the spirit of wine. Robert Parker has said that he was repeatedly invited to appear on Louis Rukeyser's *Wall Street Week* but declined every time because he knew that the host wanted to talk about wine as an investment opportunity and he found the idea anathema. Parker took an admirable stand, and the wine world owes him a debt of gratitude for his outspoken opposition to wine speculation.

But wine speculation may be a self-correcting problem at this point. Prices for the most sought-after Bordeaux, both older vintages and more recent ones, are now exorbitant—over $1,000 a bottle in good vintages—and it is hard to see them going significantly higher anytime soon. Ditto the most acclaimed Burgundies. True, Burgundy prices more accurately reflect supply and demand than Bordeaux prices; Domaine de la Romanée-Conti makes just 6,000 bottles a year of its flagship wine, called Romanée-Conti, whereas Château Latour annually pumps out nearly 200,000 bottles of its *grand vin*. Still, with Romanée-Conti selling for $5,000 a bottle in top vintages these days, it's hard to imagine that there is much additional upside for the wine. One can argue that the likes of Pétrus and Romanée-Conti are now fairly valued or overvalued; it is hard to argue that they are undervalued. And one thing that is sure to keep a lid on prices going forward is fear of fraud. The huge run-up in prices for top wines naturally created an incentive to create counterfeit bottles, and it appears that the rare-wine market has been flooded with fakes.

Although few bargains are to be found in Bordeaux and Burgundy, there is value elsewhere—not the kind of value that will yield big financial returns, but value that can deliver a lot of drinking pleasure at prices that are, relatively speaking, quite attractive. In particular, four categories of wines are arguably undervalued relative to the quality:

- *Classic California Cabernets*  Wines such as Ridge Monte Bello, Montelena Estate, and Mayacamas have been among California's standard-bearers for decades now, and they remain at the top. Bottles from the 1970s, '80s, and '90s can still be picked up for attractive prices, and current releases are reasonably priced, too.

- *Old Riojas*  Riojas from the 1940s, '50s, '60s, and '70s can be some of the earthiest, most complex and pleasurable wines around. Look for bottles from López de Heredia (still making great wines), La Rioja Alta, CVNE, Marqués de Riscal, and Marqués de Murrieta.

- *Old Barolos and Barbarescos*  The Piedmont region of Italy is a red-wine Valhalla, and few pleasures are more sublime than drinking a great old Barolo or Barbaresco. Wines from producers such as Bruno Giacosa, Giuseppe Mascarello, Bartolo Mascarello, and Giacomo Conterno are not cheap, but they are, in my view, equal in quality to the finest Burgundies and Bordeaux and sell for a fraction of the price.

- *Vintage Port*  Much of the world seems to have lost its taste for dessert wines, and vintage Port has been among the casualties. Sales are not bad, but they aren't particularly robust, and sensational vintage Ports from legendary houses like Taylor and Fonseca, both new releases and older vintages, can be had for very attractive prices these days. You can add Madeira and Sherry to this category.

All wines get old, but few wines actually improve with age. In fact, most wines are meant to be consumed on release or not long thereafter. However, a fairly sizable list of wines do reward cellaring; it includes Bordeaux, Burgundies, Rhônes, Napa Cabernets, German Rieslings, Barolos, Barbarescos, vintage Ports, and some Champagnes. By *reward*, I mean that the wines will take on greater aromatic complexity as they mature and will display a level of refinement beyond what they are capable of showing in their youth. Not every Bordeaux or Burgundy or Rhône gets better with age; in general, only the finest ones do, and how much they improve over time, and how long they will last, varies from vintage to vintage. Broadly speaking, white wines age on their acidity, red wines on their acidity and tannins (though it must be acknowledged that some of the greatest red wines of the last century came from vintages that were relatively low in acidity). Whether white or red, wines that come from warm, ripe years have the most aging potential.

To me, the most persuasive argument against costly wines is a slightly picayune one: fear of 2, 4, 6-trichloroanisole, or TCA, a chemical compound that is harmless to humans but lethal for wines. TCA is what makes a wine "corked," giving it an off-putting damp cardboard aroma and rendering it lifeless on the palate. When you hear people talking about corked wines, this is what they mean, and it is estimated that 5–10 percent of wines sealed with natural cork are tainted in this way. If it is a $10 Côtes du Rhône you bought last week, no big deal; you take it back to the store and exchange it. But if it is a 1986 Ramonet Montrachet that's been sleeping in your basement for fifteen years, you're screwed: the wine is undrinkable, and the store that sold it to you, if it is still in business, is probably not going to refund your money.

## The Wine World's Search for Closure

For an oenophile, there is no bigger buzz kill than opening a wine you've eagerly anticipated drinking and discovering that it is corked—and if you drink wine long enough, this is bound to happen to you, probably more than once. As you might imagine, lots of wine enthusiasts, and many producers, too, have long wished for an alternative to natural cork and an end to the problem of corked bottles. Those prayers have been answered: several alternative closures for wine bottles are now available. However, they are not without problems, too.

The most prevalent alternative is the screw cap, which in certain places, such as Australia and New Zealand, has overtaken natural cork. But screw caps have some serious flaws. One of the advantages of natural cork is that it permits a little oxygen to seep into the bottle, which helps wines to age well. But screw caps admit no oxygen, and as a result, the wine often shows signs of what is called reduction, which expresses itself in the form of a rotten-egg or cabbagelike aroma. (If you've ever had a "skunked" beer, it is the same smell.) Some evidence also suggests that screw caps don't hold up well over time—that they start to decay after a certain point—which would obviously be a strong disincentive for producers of fine wines (*grand cru* and *premier cru* Burgundies, classified-growth Bordeaux, and the like) to use them. A number of those producers are known to be experimenting with screw caps to see how the wines fare over the course of ten or more years. Even if the results are encouraging, it will probably be a long time before you start seeing screw caps on high-priced Burgundies and Bordeaux.

Some winemakers are bottling their wines under synthetic corks, but these have been shown to be rather poor sealants, permitting too much oxygen into the bottle. Glass stoppers are now also on the market, but they are relatively costly, which has thus far prevented them from catching on in a big way. In the meantime, there is at least some anecdotal evidence that natural cork manufacturers, faced with rising competition, have improved the reliability of their closures and that the incidence of cork taint is declining. That would seem to be the best solution of all, because natural cork really does excel as a stopper. And—call me sentimental, call me a Luddite or a flat-earther—I will also admit that I adore the sound of a popping cork; it is part of the romance of wine, and I would hate to lose it. Lose it if we must, I say, but I'd rather we do not.

## Is There a Statute of Limitations on Returning Flawed Bottles?

If I purchase a bottle from my nearby wine shop, open it tonight, and discover that it is corked, I will take it back to the store tomorrow expecting to be offered a refund or a replacement bottle, and I hope the merchant will do just that (I hate arguing in public). But what if I put the bottle in my cellar and don't open it for a year? Should the store still be willing to take it back? What if I don't pull the cork until, say, 2018?

This is an issue for which there are no regulations or guidelines; retailers make their own rules. I think it is reasonable to expect a retailer to take back an obviously corked wine within twelve months of the sale, and as long as the customer has a receipt, I see no reason why such a wine can't be returned eighteen or even twenty-four months after purchase. And it's worth pointing out that the merchant doesn't eat the cost of that damaged bottle: the cost is ultimately passed back to the winery. But after two or three years, it might be tricky to get a retailer to agree to refund the money. That doesn't necessarily mean you are out of luck. If it is a foreign wine, you might approach the importer and see if something can be done (perhaps the importer can arrange a refund or help get you a replacement bottle). If it is an American wine, you might go directly to the winery; the good ones care deeply about customer service and may well be willing to replace the bottle.

However you decide to handle the issue, you need to be sure that the bottle really is corked or otherwise damaged. If the wine just isn't to your liking, that's a tougher proposition. If you bought the wine on the recommendation of the merchant, he or she should be willing to take it back; if you bought it of your own volition, there is no obligation to do so, though a smart retailer, like a smart restaurateur, will go out of the way to make the customer happy, even if that means losing a few dollars.

4

⚬⚭⚬

# Wrath of Grapes

*W*HO SAID there is no disputing taste? For many oeno-philes, part of the pleasure of wine is arguing about it. In recent years, the wine world has seen a contentious debate over what can be called, for lack of a less ponderous phrase, first principles. What defines quality in a wine? How about authenticity? Is it ultimately more important for a wine to taste good or to taste true to its origins—to exhibit *goût de terroir*, as the French say? And if the end result is agreeable, does it matter how a wine was made? With much of the wine industry fixated on branding and marketing and technology increasingly giving vintners the power to bend nature to their will, these questions have taken on added urgency, and the discussion of them has grown ever more acrimonious, with terms such as *anti-flavor wine elite* and *spoofulated* being tossed around like hand grenades.

All this Sturm und Drang over wine can seem excessive; after all, we're talking about fermented grape juice, not war and peace. (There's that preemptive cringe I mentioned!) The rancor of some of these debates brings to mind Freud's famous comment about the

In 2010, Robert Parker took a memorable swipe at people who do not share his affection for hulking, high-alcohol Australian wines—"leg-spreaders," as the Australians like to call them. Via Twitter, he denounced these naysayers as an "anti-flavor wine elite." The phrase instantly went viral and became a rallying cry for the very people Parker had slammed. Suddenly merchants, sommeliers, and consumers whose preferences differed from Parker's and who deplored the tendency of producers to cater to his predilections had a catchphrase for their cause. It has since been trimmed to just an abbreviation—on wine sites, posters will identify themselves as AFWE.

But it was the anti-Parker forces who fired the first shot in this war of words, coining the term *spoofulated*—*spoofed* for short—to describe wines that are egregiously manipulated—made with excessive new oak, enzymes, and other additives that give them a tarted-up taste. The word was apparently conceived in New York anti-flavor wine elite circles and quickly caught on.

Whether a wine can be classified as spoofulated is obviously a subjective judgment. However, one brand of wines has become virtually synonymous with the term. Mollydooker is a line of wines produced in Australia. These are some of the most over-the-top, flamboyant, palate-searing wines you will every taste. If you can find a bottle of Mollydooker, give it a try; just don't say you weren't warned!

"narcissism of small differences." It also reminds one of Fran Lebowitz's remark that "great people talk about ideas, average people talk about things, and small people talk about wine." Small people, small differences. But as a not-infrequent combatant in these wine debates, I think they serve a useful purpose: they force people to rethink issues and to question their own assumptions, and they can often lead to improved farming and winemaking. For instance, the scrutiny that has been applied to Parker in recent years has not only yielded a more balanced and accurate assessment of his career than the hagiographic accounts that were predominant a decade ago; I think it has had a liberating effect on many winemakers, who no longer feel obliged to cater to Parker's whims.

Even as his career nears its end, Parker remains a singularly polarizing figure in the wine world. There is no denying his towering legacy; no one did more than Parker to get Americans excited about wine or to turn them on to the good stuff. However, he has become something of an irascible tyrant in his twilight, often lashing out at Burgundy, Burgundy fans, and other enemies, real or imagined. His palate, too, has undergone a peculiar evolution. Many oenophiles, as they get on in years, gravitate to quiet, subtle wines. By contrast, Parker's thirst for the big and dramatic seems only to have grown, to the point that the word *Parkerized* has become universal shorthand for ultraripe, high-alcohol, lavishly oaked wines—hedonistic fruit bombs, to use the Parker vernacular. Oak and alcohol have become two of the most contentious issues in wine, and both are worth a close look.

## OAK

Along with genuflecting in the direction of Burgundy and bad-mouthing Parker, complaining about the use of new oak is considered a mark of sophistication in some wine circles these days. Occasionally you'll even catch people griping about the oakiness of wines that weren't actually raised in oak (word to the wise: if you are going to complain about the wood influence in a wine, first make sure the wine was actually vinified and/or aged in wood). Wood barrels have long been used to age wines, but it was in the 1960s and '70s that the idea of using new barrels for each vintage took hold. Although the history is a bit murky, the use of new oak barrels seems to have caught on first in Bordeaux and then spread elsewhere, including California. Oak barrels, whether new or old, expose wines to small amounts of oxygen; the oxygen seeps in through the wood's pores and serves both to soften wines and to give them greater aromatic complexity. The difference between older barrels and new ones is that the latter often impart wood tannins to wines and can strongly influence their taste. The most fashionable barrels are made of new French oak, which can contribute sweetish flavors such as vanilla, coffee, and chocolate to wines. American oak is also popular and is known to give off flavors such as vanilla, coconut, and dill. How much flavor the barrels impart is a function of how tightly grained the wood is, how long the wood was aged, and how heavily it was toasted during the barrel-making. Putting the wine in barrels during the fermentation process can also heighten the influence of the wood.

The oak issue has been one of the biggest dividing lines in wine. In the Piedmont region of Italy, for instance, a spirited, sometimes acrimonious debate has raged over the past two decades between so-called modernist producers and more traditional winemakers, and the use of new oak has been at the center of it. The modernists age their Barolos and Barbarescos in new French oak barrels rather than the large Slovenian oak casks that have customarily been used for these Nebbiolo-based wines. Most critics seem to like the new oak influence, but many Nebbiolo aficionados deplore it. Likewise, oak has figured prominently in the recent history of Spain's Rioja region. Riojas were traditionally aged in American oak, but in recent years most Rioja producers have switched to French oak. In fact, only a couple of producers are still making traditional Riojas, much to the chagrin of some wine enthusiasts, myself among them.

New oak, applied judiciously, can add complexity to a wine without being obtrusive. Burgundy's Domaine de la Romanée-Conti, for instance, uses new oak for almost all its wines, but the oak influence is remarkably discreet. With other wines it is not nearly so subtle—the oak dominates the aroma, and the wood tannins can leave you feeling like you've got splinters in your tongue. A lot of California Cabernets and Merlots wear their oak heavily, as do some newer-style Bordeaux. Parker has lavished huge praise on many of these wines, and while he would surely dispute the idea that he is drawn to new oak flavors, he clearly doesn't mind them. His fondness for these oaky wines has led many producers to ratchet up their use of new wood. However, this trend can't be attributed solely to Parker's influence. It seems a lot of consumers enjoy oakiness, too, which is why you find a number of mass-market producers using oak chips in their wines—a cheaper method than buying expensive barrels, and one that also imparts a strong oak influence.

The good news, if you are not a fan of oaky wines, is that more and more producers seem to be backing off on the oak. Partly it's an economic decision: new oak barrels are expensive, and with the economy still recovering and wine buyers being more selective and budget-minded, it's hard to pass that cost along to consumers. But it's also aesthetic: more people are gravitating to wines that are made with a lighter touch in the cellar, to wines that show the influence of the vineyard more than the influence of the barrel, and a growing number of producers no longer feel so pressured to cater to the predilections of oak-happy critics. Oak barrels will undoubtedly remain a staple in many wine regions, but they may not be quite as pervasive as they were before.

## ALCOHOL

Wine wouldn't be wine without the alcohol, and the buzz it delivers is part of the pleasure. But alcohol levels have been climbing, much to the chagrin of some oenophiles, who find higher-octane wines overbearing and exhausting to drink. Fermentation converts the sugar in grapes into alcohol. Sugar is a function of ripeness, and the more sugar there is in the grapes, the more alcohol you end up with in the wine. Alcohol, in addition to getting you mellow, adds body, texture, and a perception of sweetness to wines, and as the alcohol content increases, wines become thicker, heavier, and sweeter. Grapes such as Zinfandel and Grenache naturally yield wines that are fairly high in alcohol, as do warmer regions like the southern Rhône and the Barossa Valley. But alcohol levels have been rising in a number of places, such as Bordeaux, that historically have produced restrained, modestly alcoholic wines, threatening the character of the local wines.

California has become the main flash point in the debate over alcohol. Visit any wine shop and you'll quickly see why: the shelves are groaning with California wines in excess of 14 or even 15 percent alcohol, and the labels may not even be telling the full story. Under U.S. law, wines 14 percent or under can vary as much as 1.5 percent from what is stated on the label, as long as the actual content does not surpass 14 percent, and those above 14 percent are permitted a 1 percent margin of error. Although California has always produced its share of floozies,

Napa Cabernets and Merlots generally weren't as heady in the past. A study led by University of California Davis professor Julian Alston found that sugar levels in California grapes have jumped 9 percent since 1980.

What accounts for the spike? Climate change is often cited, and it certainly appears to be a factor in other regions. But Alston and his colleagues suggested that the higher sugar levels in California were mainly the result of farming practices. They speculated that different rootstocks and new planting systems may have had a role, and they also raised another possibility: producers harvest riper fruit in order to craft wines that appeal to critics, namely Parker. They noted that the largest sugar increases have been for premium grapes—Cabernet, Merlot, Chardonnay—and in premium areas such as Napa and Sonoma. They wrote that this "could be consistent with a 'Parker effect' . . . of wineries responding to market demand and seeking riper-flavored, more intense wines."

Parker has wielded extraordinary influence, and his California scores have long indicated a weakness not just for new oak but for ultraripe (read: high alcohol) wines. His words, too. Some years ago he blasted Tim Mondavi, Robert's son, for making wines that he considered too light and restrained. He accused Mondavi of "going against what Mother Nature has given California" and said that the strength of California wines "lies in power, exuberance, and gloriously ripe fruit." In 2007 he launched a similar diatribe against California vintner Steve Edmunds. "What Steve is doing appears to be a deliberate attempt to make French-styled wines," he sneered. "If you want to make French wine, do it in France." Considering the power of Parker's ratings, it would stand to reason that many producers took the unsubtle hints and made sure to deliver the kind of wines he favored.

Parker's thirst for hedonistic fruit bombs, as he calls them, extends to Pinot Noir. In Burgundy, where Pinot is the signature red grape, the cool northerly climate makes ripeness a challenge, and as a result, the wines tend to be modest in alcohol. But with Parker's blessing (or prodding), California Pinot has evolved in a very different direction: the wines are often very ripe and lush, with alcohol levels pushing or even topping 15 percent. Echoing Parker, proponents of this style contend that it is a natural expression of California's sun-splashed *terroir* and that comparisons with Burgundy are misguided. Apples to oranges, they say.

There's some truth to that. It is silly (and unrealistic) to think that California Pinots should taste like red Burgundies, and for diversity's sake, we shouldn't want them to taste indistinguishable from Burgundies. But they should at least taste like Pinot Noirs, and the problem with the high-alcohol Pinots is that the varietal character is often extinguished by the overripe fruit—to the point that a lot of these bruisers taste more like Syrah than Pinot. Another problem with the overripe style is that it tends to overwhelm the influence of the vineyard. Pinot is particularly adept at capturing the "voice" of the soil, at conveying *terroir*—site expression is what Burgundy is all about—and to lose that quality is to lose a big part of what makes Pinot such a great grape.

But I also recognize that this is an issue that mostly concerns hardened oenophiles and that much of the wine-buying public is not nearly so persnickety when it comes to Pinot and other wines. For instance, another gripe about full-throttle wines is that they can be tough to match with food, which is true: the flip side of all that alcohol is that the wines tend to be low in palate-cleansing acidity. For fusspots like me, that's a big problem, but for many casual wine enthusiasts, it may not be an issue. A survey a few years ago found that most of the wine consumed in the United States is not drunk with meals. Instead, wine is mainly used as a cocktail beverage. The news came as a cold shower to some alcohol agonizers, and that was a good thing: it was a reminder that our preferences are not everyone's preferences. The fact is, a lot of consumers enjoy buxom wines, Pinot and otherwise, and I can't fault producers for giving these people what they want. If I'm getting the kinds of wines that I like and other people are getting the kind they like, it is all good.

## CRUNCHY WINES

All that said, we are now seeing a movement away from the fruit bombs that Parker favors and toward more elegant, *terroir*-driven wines. Not surprisingly, there is also a growing emphasis on eco-friendly farming practices and on ensuring that vineyards are tended in an environmentally sound and sustainable way. Interest in winemaking practices has increased as well. Vintners can now manipulate the flavor, texture, and color of wines in all sorts of ways; while these practices are safe, there is a lot of discussion about whether they constitute a form of cheating. Two big movements have sprung up in recent years that deal with these issues in one way or another.

## BIODYNAMIC VITICULTURE

Why are some of the world's most eminent winemakers filling cow horns with cow dung and burying them in their vineyards, stuffing animal skulls with grated oak bark and burying these, too, in the dirt, and consulting astrological calendars to determine when to harvest their grapes? More important, why are these bizarre practices, prescribed in 1924 by a teetotalist Austrian philosopher, yielding such excellent wines? That's the mystery, and controversy, at the heart of biodynamic winemaking, an ultraorganic, deeply ideological approach to viticulture that is winning the adherence of top wine producers on both sides of the Atlantic. But it has also drawn the wrath of the scientific community, which is convinced that biodynamics is little more than a cultish fraud. There is a cultish quality to it. But as always with wine, the ultimate test is in the glass, and right now the evidence is pretty compelling: all that interred cow shit seems to be producing superior Cabernets and Chardonnays.

Three of Burgundy's most celebrated estates, Domaine de la Romanée-Conti, Domaine Leroy, and Domaine Leflaive, have gone biodynamic. So has Zind-Humbrecht in Alsace, Michel Chapoutier and Beaucastel in the Rhône Valley, and Louis Roederer in Champagne. Closer to home, Araujo Estate Wines, which makes one of Napa's most sought-after Cabernets, has embraced the biodynamic approach, as has Joseph Phelps, a legendary Napa winery. Each week seems to bring word of a new heavyweight convert to biodynamic viticulture. What was until fairly recently a fringe movement has become the biggest sensation to hit the wine world since the emergence of Parker.

Biodynamic viticulture traces its origins to a series of lectures delivered in 1924 by the Viennese scholar Rudolf Steiner. In a city famed for its intellectual vitality, Steiner distinguished himself both for the breadth and depth of his interests and knowledge and for the peculiarity of many of the ideas he espoused. He is best known as the father of anthroposophy, a convoluted doctrine that seeks to examine the spiritual world by means of the same scientific methods used to explore the physical universe and that aims to help the individual transcend materialism in order to

69

forge closer ties with fellow humans, with nature, and with his own soul. The philosophy has attracted some prominent adherents and admirers over the years, including Franz Kafka and Saul Bellow, and it also serves as the basis for the Waldorf education movement (also known as Steiner education), which flourishes to this day.

In 1924, Steiner gave a series of lectures in Germany in which he laid out what became the core tenets of biodynamic agriculture. Steiner, in his early sixties at the time and in failing health (he died the following year), was asked by a group of farmers in Silesia (now part of Poland) to help them find a way of reversing the declining quality of their soils and crops, a crisis that they attributed to the use of chemical fertilizers and pesticides. It was an issue that had long concerned Steiner, who often lamented how much poorer fruits, vegetables, and meats had become during his lifetime, a downturn he blamed on industrialized agriculture. In response to the farmers' urgent request, Steiner traveled to Germany and delivered eight lectures prescribing not just a remedy for their problems but a new, revolutionary approach to agriculture. He told the farmers to stop using chemicals in their fields. In this, he was doing nothing more than embracing a central precept of organic farming. But what he went on to suggest would set biodynamic agriculture apart from mere organic farming. In Steiner's schemata, the farm was not simply an incubator of life but an organism itself, in which everything was intrinsically connected to everything else. A sick chicken had repercussions for the tomatoes; a diseased tree was a problem for the cows. Likewise, said Steiner, each farm was part of a larger biosystem; the earth itself was an organism, and it was clearly linked, gravitationally and otherwise, to the sun, the moon, and the other planets.

Steiner's theory of agricultural management was an odd amalgam of the autarkic and the universal (the cosmic, really). He proposed that each farm essentially be walled off from the rest of the world—that it be operated as an entirely self-sustaining entity, devoid of outside influences of any kind. This would require, among other things, using homemade fertilizers and pesticides, and Steiner instructed farmers to employ a specific array of homeopathic preparations, which he numbered 500 through 508. Preparation 500, for instance, was meant to promote healthy soil and involved filling a cow's horn with cow manure, burying it in the field in the autumn, and exhuming it in the spring. Preparation 506, a compost, required placing dandelion flowers in the stomach lining of a cow; this was to be planted in the earth during the winter months and dug up in the spring. For rodent control, Steiner turned to the skies: he prescribed catching a young field mouse, skinning it, burning the skin, and spreading the ashes across the field when the planet Venus occults the Scorpio constellation. He also instructed the farmers to plant their crops and harvest them according to planetary alignments. He claimed that the position of the moon and the other planets had a clear, demonstrable impact on all phases of a plant's development and that only by getting in sync with the rhythms of the solar system could the farmers restore their farms to health and improve the quality of their crops.

In 1981, Nicolas Joly, a young winemaker in the Loire, found a book about biodynamics at a secondhand store and took it with him on a skiing holiday. Entranced, he reread the book several times before returning home. Joly had recently taken over his family's winery, Clos de la Coulée de Serrant, a legendary domaine set on the Loire River a few minutes outside the town of Angers. Coulée de Serrant is part of the Savennières appellation and produces a wine by that name, made from the Chenin Blanc grape. Coulée de Serrant's Savennières was once among the most esteemed French wines; the celebrated food writer Curnonsky famously declared it to be one of the five great white wines of France. Although the wines of Savennières had since fallen out of fashion, eclipsed in popularity by more opulent Chardonnay-based wines, Coulée de Serrant remained one of the most recognized names in French viticulture.

Joly stumbled upon the book at a time when he was experiencing a crisis in the vineyard. He had been using chemical treatments for several years, and like Steiner's Silesian farmers, he had watched as the quality of his soil and of his wines steadily eroded. To discover at that moment a book that perfectly described the problems he faced and a method of farming custom-designed to combat those problems was fortuitous beyond words. But for Joly, the biodynamic approach wasn't attractive simply because it promised to restore his vines to health; he also found its philosophical underpinnings appealing. Joly had just left a career as an investment banker (he holds an MBA from Columbia and worked for several years in New York) to take over Coulée de Serrant. But familial duty was not the only thing that brought him back to the Loire: he had grown disillusioned with finance and numbers and conventional modes of thinking and living. He was open to new ways of looking at the world, and he found in Steiner and biodynamics a tonic not just for his vineyard but for his soul.

Joly fully converted Coulée de Serrant to biodynamism in 1984. Today he is its most outspoken and militant advocate within the wine world. His book, *Wine from Sky to Earth*, a combination how-to guide and philosophic meditation, is considered the ur-text of biodynamic viticulture (in the dedication, Joly credits

Steiner's writings with giving "profound meaning to my life"). He organizes large tastings of biodynamic wines in cities around the world and uses these events as a chance to preach to the converted and proselytize to the uninitiated. His style is unfailingly charmless and hectoring. An evangelical and missionary, he believes that biodynamism offers the only path to good wine. He also contends that the world is on the brink of environmental apocalypse and that embracing biodynamic viticulture is no longer merely a choice; it is a moral imperative ("We have reached the time when nature will implement its law on earth").

Ironically, while the biodynamic approach appears to be yielding better wines almost everywhere that it is applied, it seems to have taken Coulée de Serrant in reverse. In fact, it is widely agreed that under Joly's management, Coulée de Serrant's Savennières has become a stinker. That has been my experience: I have consistently found Joly's wines to be ungenerous oddballs, emitting off-putting aromas and flavors. For Joly, the result seems to be a secondary concern; what apparently matters most is the process. "Before it can be good," he has said, "a wine must be true." Likewise, his book includes this nugget: "A biodynamic wine is not necessarily 'good,' but it is always *authentic*."

Joly, with his fire-and-brimstone style, is a fat target for biodynamics skeptics, of which there are many. A lot of people regard the method as New Age hooey. Stu Smith of California's Smith-Madrone winery, which makes some of the best wines you have probably never heard of, thinks that Steiner was a kook and that the biodynamic method is "a hoax" that ought to be accorded "the same level of respect we give witchcraft." He has even set up a website called biodynamicsisahoax.com. In an article for the magazine *World of Fine Wine*, Douglass Smith and

Jesús Barquín (the former a New York investor and wine collector with a doctorate in the history of science, the latter a Spanish wine expert and professor of criminology) dismissed the biodynamic approach as "a vista of starry eyes and good intentions mixed with quasi-religious hocus-pocus, good salesmanship, and plain scientific illiteracy." They pointed out that there is no evidence that biodynamics yields healthier soils and grapes than regular organic viticulture and suggested that its positive effects are almost surely attributable to the standard organic practices it employs (no chemical fertilizers or pesticides are used). Indeed, they said, the few credible studies that have been done comparing the effects of biodynamics and organic viticulture on soil and grapes found no statistically significant differences between the two approaches. They ridiculed Steiner's eight preparations as "viticultural voodoo" and savaged the cosmological aspects of biodynamics as "pseudoscience." In their judgment, biodynamics was nothing more than faith-based farming.

The faith-based aspect is undeniable. Like many faiths, biodynamics even has a schism. The main biodynamic organization, Demeter International, which was founded in 1928, certifies all types of biodynamic farms. Several years ago, a handful of French biodynamic winemakers, frustrated by Demeter's global mandate and what they viewed as its lax standards, formed a breakaway group called Biodivin, which certifies only biodynamic wineries. The U.S. arm of Demeter responded by trademarking the name Biodynamic, thus preventing American wineries from using the word *biodynamic* on their labels unless authorized to do so by Demeter.

So what to make of biodynamics? Even if some of it amounts to quackery, it yields seriously good wines, and the fact that it has won the adherence of some of the foremost producers on the planet speaks to the quality of the results. Not all biodynamic wines are good—just look at Coulée de Serrant. But the good ones, and there are many of them, are not only delicious; they display a vigor that you don't typically find in wines made from conventionally farmed grapes. There is an almost feral intensity about them, an untamed aspect that makes them seem somehow closer to the vine, closer to the vineyard. Like Stu Smith and other biodynamic bashers, I'm skeptical of Steiner and can't help but roll my eyes at the preparations that he prescribed. I suspect that the real secret behind the success of biodynamics is that it encourages—requires, really—winemakers to take fanatical care of their vineyards. By eschewing the use of all chemicals and painstakingly nurturing their vines and the soils beneath them, biodynamic producers are able to obtain great fruit (assuming the weather cooperates), which translates into fantastic wines assuming they show a reasonably deft hand in the cellar. I'm not sold on the particulars of biodynamics, but the quality of the wines has made a believer of me.

## NATURAL WINES

Among oenophiles of all persuasions—those who enjoy fruit bombs, those who prefer less percussive wines—it is an article of faith that winemaking is best done with a light touch. We grape nuts never tire of pointing out that wine is foremost an agricultural product, and wine nomenclature, with its surfeit of pastoral imagery, underscores this essential fact. It is considered axiomatic that the best wines are those that bear the fewest fingerprints and that most clearly reflect the particular attributes of their vineyards—that offer the least adulterated expressions of sun, soil, and vine possible. In recent decades, however, science has given vintners an array of tools that can be used to change the fundamental character of a wine, altering its color, structure, texture, and taste. Inferior land, bad weather, and shoddy farming are no longer necessarily impediments to producing appealing wines; using technology, winemakers can now override the will of nature and perform all kinds of nips and tucks on their Cabernets and Syrahs.

The natural wine movement began as a backlash against this kind of manipulation. The idea was to defend authenticity and artisanship against industrial winemaking and bland homogeneity. Although using the word *natural* in reference to food or drink is normally taken to be an implicit claim of wholesomeness, health concerns have never factored prominently in the natural-wine canon, nor could they. That's because there is no evidence that "unnatural" practices—using additives such as powdered tannins, for instance, or oak chips—are harmful to consumers. They won't rot your innards, cause your teeth to fall out, or reduce your sperm count. The argument against them is simply that they represent a form of cheating and yield less authentic wines.

But it is one thing to want wines to be made as naturally as possible; it is quite another to anoint certain wines as "natural," and this is where the natural-wine movement runs into a wall of tannins. For one thing, a truly natural wine goes by another name: it is called vinegar. If you don't add sulfur dioxide, which acts as an antioxidant and preservative, during the vinification process, the wine will very likely spoil and become vinegar (more on sulfur in a moment). So what then do natural-wine proponents really mean when they talk about "natural" wines? That's not entirely clear. In contrast to biodynamic wines, for which there are certification programs that require adherence to prescribed farming practices, natural wines have no official classification, no sanctioning body that decrees whether a wine qualifies.

In broadest terms, "natural" wines are described as those that have been made with minimal involvement by the vintner. As with organic and biodynamic wines, the grapes must come from vineyards that have not been treated with synthetic chemicals; what sets natural wines apart is that the same hands-off approach is supposed to be carried into the cellar. The winemaker performs only those tasks that require midwifery, such as crushing the fruit. Apart from that, the wines are left to birth themselves; "nothing added, nothing taken away" is the popular catchphrase. This means relying on ambient yeasts—those floating around the cellar and vineyard—rather than commercial ones, eschewing high-tech toys such as spinning cones and reverse osmosis machines, and neither acidifying wines nor otherwise tinkering with their composition.

But when you move beyond these general guidelines, the natural-wine idea devolves into a conceptual free-for-all. Take, for instance, the issue of sulfur dioxide. Some naturalistas insist that sulfur should never be added, vinegar be damned; others say it is permissible but only in small amounts (some cap it at 10 milligrams per liter total $SO_2$, others say up to 20, but many refuse to put a number on it). Then there is chaptalization, the process of adding sugar before or during fermentation in order to boost a wine's alcohol content. Hardliners consider it verboten, but others, no doubt mindful of the long tradition of chaptalization in natural-wine strongholds like France's Beaujolais region, are more flexible.

There even appears to be wiggle room on the all-important yeast question. Strict constructionists assert that manufactured yeasts aren't allowed under any circumstances; use them and you forfeit the right to call yours a natural wine. But other people say that you can employ them if it's the only way to finish fermenting a wine. Some natural-wine evangelists contend that beyond certain inviolable principles—not using poisons in the vineyard, for instance—intent matters as much as actions; if a vintner is making a good-faith effort to be natural, that's good enough.

I'd be more inclined to take this movement seriously if the wines were unequivocally superior, but that's not the case. Some of them are great. The late Marcel Lapierre's Morgon, a *cru* Beaujolais that was widely regarded as a beacon of naturalness, was consistently ethereal—in fact, I can't think of a wine that made me happier. The wines imported by New York–based Louis/Dressner are likewise considered paragons of minimalism and are usually delicious. However, plenty of mediocre wines are also parading under the natural banner, and a lot of hideously bad ones are, too—oxidized, microbial messes that only a vintner's mother, or an ideologue who values means over ends, could possibly love.

And here's a related point: nonintervention can often be more detrimental to *terroir* expression and authenticity than intervention. If, for instance, a vintner chooses not to add sulfur to his wine and the wine oxidizes or is otherwise flawed, he has actually throttled the voice of the vineyard. Oxidation is not an expression of *terroir*; it is inimical to the expression of it (a point that Paul Draper, arguably America's finest winemaker and a longtime practitioner of minimal intervention, has made). If the goal of "natural" wines is to produce wines that taste true to their origins, then eschewing the use of sulfur makes no sense; if the result is an oxidized wine, it is a wine that reflects the cellar practices of the winemaker more than the particular attributes of the vineyard from which it came.

Given the growing influence of science and technology over wine, a backlash was inevitable, and for now the backlash has taken the form of the natural-wine movement. Natural advocates are driven in part by a romanticized view of the past: that if only we could go back to the way that wines used to be made, our palates would be so much better off. But this is mythologizing on an epic scale. Forget ancient wines and just focus on the more recent past. Fifty years ago, a lot of wines were quite literally dirty—they were made in filthy cellars and were often riddled with flaws. Why did new oak barrels became fashionable in Bordeaux in the 1960s and '70s? Because the great consulting oenologist Émile Peynaud pointed out that the use of dirty old barrels teeming with bacteria had fatally compromised many wines, and he managed to persuade winemakers to start using cleaner wood and otherwise to improve the hygiene in their cellars. Sure, the new oak thing has gone too far, but the use of sanitary wood vessels for aging wines helped raise the quality not only in Bordeaux but throughout the wine world. These days clean, stable wines are the norm, and that is a significant and wholly salutary change from fifty or a hundred years ago.

That said, I'm all in favor of experimentation, and if the natural-wine movement encourages people to give more thought to how they vinify their grapes, that's a good thing. I can also say that I share the same general outlook as natural-wine proponents. I don't want wines doctored up by machines and chemical additives in order to invest them with qualities they would otherwise lack, even if those artificial influences aren't necessarily obvious to my palate. But for the same reason that I prefer clean sports stars to those who are bulked up on steroids, I want wines that come by their attributes as naturally as possible. I'll take Hank Aaron wines over Barry Bonds wines any day.

But I think "natural" advocates ought to ditch the "natural" label, which is hopelessly tendentious and polarizing, and instead put the focus where it really belongs, on individual wines and winemakers. Call them good wines, call them distinctive, soulful, or funky wines—just don't call them natural wines.

# 5

———— ⊙ℛℛ⊙ ————

# Food and Wine,
# or Is It Food versus Wine?

*H*ERE IS ONE of the great wine ironies of our time: never have sommeliers been more prominent than they are today, and never have food and wine pairings mattered less. In case you haven't noticed, sommeliers have become the cool kids of the wine world; they are widely seen as the guys (and gals) with the best jobs in wine and the most glamorous lives. They are being celebrated in both print and film, are often as big an attraction at restaurants as the chefs (or bigger ones), and have become genuine tastemakers, too. If sommeliers get behind a particular grape or style of wine, it inevitably becomes the new "it" wine among avant-garde oenophiles. And yet all this sommelier worship comes at a time when the most basic function of sommeliers—to help diners find the right wine to match with the food they've ordered—is not nearly as important as it used to be. In part that's because of the kinds of foods we are eating these days and how those dishes are being served. It also speaks to the very self-confident wine culture that has taken root in the United States. Many people have no trouble navigating wine lists and thus have little need for advice from sommeliers.

Given the way celebrity has infected American food culture, turning chefs into television stars and cultural icons, it was probably inevitable that something similar would happen in wine. But it is curious that the spotlight has fallen on sommeliers. Without in any way intending to slight sommeliers—some of my best friends in the wine business are sommeliers—their job is not, on its face, particularly glamorous; they are wine waiters. And yet the fickle gaze of celebrity has now fallen on them, a point underscored rather dramatically by a recent documentary entitled *Somm*, which follows several sommeliers as they take the notoriously challenging Master Sommelier exam. Not only did *Somm* get screened at the 2013 Santa Barbara International Film Festival; immediately thereafter, Samuel Goldwyn Films acquired North American rights to it. And with that, the celebrity sommelier phenomenon reached the ultimate destination, Hollywood.

While it is easy to be snarky about all this sommelier worship, the rise of the American sommelier is actually a very interesting story. Although the role of wine waiter did not originate in France—it apparently dates back to the Greeks and Romans—the job took its modern form there, which was good in some respects, not so good in others. On the plus side, the French invested the otherwise ho-hum business of opening and pouring wine with ceremony and élan. On the down side, they brought a pronounced hauteur to the task. Many French sommeliers came to the job not by choice but by conscription, and the position has usually been a life sentence. In France, the sommelier was often someone who entered the restaurant trade as a barely pubescent teen with dreams of becoming a chef (and no prospect of attending university). Then, deemed unworthy of a place at the stove, our man—and it was always a man—got shunted off to the wine cellar, where he was condemned to spend the rest of his working days in the shadow of the egomaniacal prick who beat him out in the kitchen. This was not a recipe for service with a smile.

By contrast, professional wine service in the United States is a relatively recent phenomenon—it only really started in the 1980s—and took root in very different fashion. The pioneering figures here—Kevin Zraly (Windows on the World), Daniel Johnnes (Montrachet), Larry Stone (Charlie Trotter's, Rubicon)—were all college-educated and came to wine out of passion, not because they were frog-marched into the bottle room. They saw their role as mainly pedagogical, an outlook perfectly tailored to a time when Americans were developing an interest in wine. They made wine service educational, and they made it fun. They also brought an entrepreneurial spirit to the work. Rather than let the role of sommelier define them, they defined it, turning a dead-end, white-men-only métier into an exemplar of upward mobility and diversity.

Consider, for instance, Johnnes, now (along with Stone) the dean of American sommeliers. In 1985, Drew Nieporent put him in charge of the wine service at Montrachet, a restaurant he was opening in New York. Johnnes, taking his inspiration from the restaurant's name—Montrachet is the grandest of *grand cru* white Burgundies—assembled a spectacular cellar, and he and the wine list became the restaurant's star attractions (not that the food wasn't also good). In the late '80s, Johnnes began bringing in some of the unknown wines that he had discovered on trips to

France. Today he has a thriving import business with a roster full of impressive names, oversees wine operations for chef Daniel Boulud's restaurant group, and has even done some winemaking himself: a few years ago, he produced a small amount of red Burgundy with the help of Frédéric Mugnier, one of the region's most esteemed *vignerons*, and made an Oregon Pinot Noir with the assistance of the talented Eric Hamacher. In addition to all this, Johnnes organizes what has become in the eyes of many people the world's greatest wine event, La Paulée de New York, a bacchanal modeled after the annual postharvest festival in Meursault. (It is actually a bicoastal event now, alternating each year between New York and San Francisco.)

Younger sommeliers are following the same trajectory. Indian-born Rajat Parr originally made a name for himself on the San Francisco wine scene. These days he oversees wine service for all chef Michael Mina's restaurants. He is also producing highly acclaimed Pinot Noirs and Chardonnays from California's Central Coast—his label is known as Sandhi—and has become a de facto leader in the movement to bring greater restraint and finesse to California wines. He was one of the founders of an organization called In Pursuit of Balance, which promotes this new paradigm through seminars and tastings. Parr has also written a book; a few years ago he coauthored with wine writer Jordan Mackay a book called *Secrets of the Sommeliers*, which combined practical advice for consumers with an inside look at the fabulous life of sommeliers. And no sommelier leads a more fabulous existence than Parr. His Twitter feed, under the handle RN74 (RN74 is a wine-focused restaurant in San Francisco that's part of the Michael Mina empire and which takes its name from the main north-south route in Burgundy; there's a Seattle branch now, too), ought to be titled "Travels with Raj." Every week seems to find Parr in a different city or wine region; one week it's New York, the next it is Piedmont, the week after that it is Paris, Tokyo, or points in between, and invariably with pictures of the amazing wines he's consumed. Yes, Raj has quite the life.

What many sommeliers will tell you is that all this entrepreneurship and diversification is motivated in part by necessity. Wine service is a young person's game; working the dining room floor night after night takes its toll after ten or fifteen years, especially if you have a family, and so sommeliers need to find different ways of putting their skills and knowledge to use. In this sense, they are like veteran chefs who open multiple restaurants, establish product lines, and so forth. Obviously, part of the motivation for these chefs is a determination to cash in on the renown that they've achieved, but it is also prompted by a desire to step away from the stove after years of toiling in kitchens.

But while sommeliers are more visible than ever, how much value do they really add to the dining experience? For one thing, sommeliers are generally found at high-end restaurants, and a lot of high-end cooking has become so eclectic that it is almost pointless to try to create appropriate wine pairings. Some of today's most influential chefs—Ferran Adrià of the recently closed El Bulli in Spain, Heston Blumenthal of the Fat Duck outside London, and Grant Achatz of Alinea in Chicago, to name three of the most celebrated among them—have a wildly inventive streak that, whatever its virtues, can fall a little short when it comes to wine compatibility. What exactly do you pair with, say, coconut ravioli in soy sauce, or a Parmesan cheese ice cream sandwich, two of Adrià's dishes? Or how about sea urchin with frozen banana, puffed rice, and parsnip milk, an Achatz dish?

Obviously, these are extreme examples, and I'm certainly not suggesting that chefs should restrain their creative impulses on account of wine. I'm merely pointing out that the trendiest cooking these days does not necessarily lend itself to straightforward wine pairings (or any wine pairings at all). And the problem isn't limited to the most outré cooking; even more mainstream restaurants are using so many eclectic/exotic ingredients now that matching wines to these preparations can be migraine-inducing. Sommeliers would argue that the fusion trend makes their presence in the dining room even more vital—that the diner needs help from someone who understands how, say, the Asiatic spices in a dish will interact with different wines. I'm not so sure that's true. Many of these dishes have such a broad spectrum of flavors that it is almost pointless to try to find that one "right" wine; they go with nothing and everything.

Another major food trend also calls into question the need for sommeliers: the rise of the tasting menu. Sure, tasting menus have been around for a long time, but in recent years they have become ubiquitous. Nowadays every ambitious chef offers a ten- or twelve-dish tasting menu, and at some restaurants the tasting menu is the only option. This has lately provoked a backlash among some food critics, who resent these "hostage" menus and the four- or five-hour time commitment they require. But there's another reason to regret this trend: in general, tasting menus aren't particularly wine-friendly. One wine is not likely to work for all the courses, nor is it really practical to change wines with each new course (the wine-by-the-glass thing can get to be insanely expensive, and drinking ten or twelve glasses of wine during a meal is not a good idea). Here, too, sommeliers would respond that this is exactly the kind of situation in which a smart, creative sommelier is needed. I'm not convinced. With so many dishes and different flavors landing on the table, the diner can probably just pick a half-bottle of white, a half-bottle of red, and do just as well.

And this leads to the most important point of all: a lot of restaurant-goers don't need help from a sommelier. Generally speaking, the kinds of people who patronize restaurants that are likely to employ sommeliers possess enough wine knowledge these days that they don't really need input from a sommelier. As long as you give them a smart, well-chosen wine list—and you certainly don't need a full-time sommelier to put together such a list—they can handle the rest.

So is there anything sommeliers are good for these days? Yes, there is: they excel at turning people on to new wines. A first-rate sommelier can introduce you to an up-and-coming producer and can acquaint you with an unfamiliar region or style of wine. That's an important function, but a good retailer does the same thing (and you don't have to buy a fancy lunch or dinner to get the advice from a retailer).

### TIPS FOR HAVING A HAPPY WINE EXPERIENCE IN A RESTAURANT

- If a restaurant makes its wine list available online, try to take a look at it beforehand; forewarned is forearmed.
- It also helps to know the retail price of wines you may be considering. Back in prehistoric times—that is to say, up until a few years ago—that was often a difficult thing to do. But with a smartphone in every pocket these days, discreetly doing some price-checking while perusing a wine list is easy and will help you avoid getting gouged.
- If a wine list is obscenely priced, order the cheapest wine

on the list simply to spite the restaurant, or better still, drink water or beer with your meal. You might even make your displeasure known.

- It is always nice to offer the sommelier or server a taste if the wine happens to be really good. With a Macon-Villages, the gesture wouldn't be necessary (though it would surely be appreciated); with a Corton-Charlemagne, it would be a very nice thing to do, particularly if the service is good.

- If you encounter a sommelier with a bad attitude, don't hesitate to call him or her out in a calm, conciliatory way. In general, restaurant wine service has never been better, but some dining room wine tyrants are still around, and they can make your evening miserable. It is a problem that needs to be dealt with the moment it rears its head.

- If you are inclined to let the sommelier choose the wine for you, make sure to let him or her know the price you are willing to pay. Good sommeliers will pick up on even the subtlest hints and make sure you drink well without paying more than you wish to.

- Try to avoid ordering wines by the glass. The prices are often astronomical, and you have no way of knowing how long the bottle has been open.

- One frequently encountered problem in restaurants is overpouring. Sometimes it is done purely by accident or because the person serving the wine doesn't know any better. More often, though, it is done deliberately; the idea is that the more the server puts in your glass at the start, the more you are apt to drink and the likelier you are to order a second bottle. My solution to this problem is what might be called the two-strikes-and-you're-out rule. If the waiter pours too much wine in the glass or is too quick with refills, I'll gently indicate that I'd like him to back off; if the problem persists, I will relieve him of the pouring duties while trying to be tactful about it. This strategy generally works well.

## BYO

Few topics get oenophiles quite as exercised as the issue of BYO, or Bring Your Own—bringing your own bottle of wine to a restaurant. Many restaurants let diners do this; those that do usually charge what's called a corkage fee, and some impose limits on how many bottles you can bring. Others permit diners to bring in only wines that aren't on the restaurant's wine list. But a lot of restaurants don't allow BYO under any circumstances, which greatly irritates many wine drinkers, who seem to think that all restaurants should allow it. I do BYO whenever I can; it enables me to drink a better wine than if I ordered off the list, and even with the corkage, it is usually more economical (a bottle that costs me $60 at retail is probably $120–$180 on most wine lists, and even with a $30 or $40 corkage fee, I'm coming out well ahead). That said, I understand why restaurants don't allow BYO or seek to limit it. Restaurants make most of their money on alcohol sales, and if they permit diners to drink their own wines, they are obviously hurting their bottom lines. I also think that if a restaurant cares enough about wine to put together a thoughtful, appealing wine list, it should be rewarded for its effort, so long as the prices are fair. That last point is a key one: if restaurants don't want to allow BYO, that's fine, but they need to limit their markups. I find few things more annoying than going to a restaurant that doesn't permit BYO and that charges extortionate prices for its wines. In such cases I'll usually drink something other than wine and will make a mental note to never come back.

### SOME FOOD AND WINE PAIRING TIPS

- Champagne and sushi is a great combination.
- Champagne and lobster is sensational, too, and deliciously decadent.
- In fact, Champagne is arguably the most versatile wine of all; it can even work with red meat. The great economist John Maynard Keynes said his one regret in life was that he didn't drink enough Champagne. One way of avoiding that problem (and it is a problem I am certainly attempting to avoid) is to drink Champagne more often with meals. What you will find is that good bubbly is a great food wine. And it doesn't just have to be Champagne: Excellent Spanish Cavas, Italian Proseccos, and American sparkling wines go equally with food and can be had for $15 or $16, a fraction of the price of even a good nonvintage Champagne.
- The better the wine, the simpler the food should be. Sure, a bottle of '89 Haut-Brion deserves to be paired with something a little more refined than, say, a ham sandwich, but if the intent is to showcase the wine, don't go for overly elaborate or heavily spiced food.
- Above all, don't drive yourself nuts trying to find ideal food and wine pairings. In most cases, there is no such thing as an ideal pairing, and good enough is, well, good enough.

- In general, wines that are lower in alcohol—say, under 14 percent—and have good acidity do better with food than high-alcohol, low-acidity wines. The acidity is especially important: it refreshes the palate between bites.
- Rieslings, particularly slightly sweet German Rieslings, are often recommended as good wines for spicy foods. That's true to a certain extent; the sweetness does parry the spice.
- If you are having barbecue or hamburgers or even fried chicken, you can go with a heftier red—something like a Zinfandel or Australian Shiraz. Those big wines do a better job of soaking up all the fat and grease than daintier reds.

## What Goes with Asian Food?

A few years ago I attended a Sauternes lunch held at an Indian restaurant in New York. Sauternes is the great sweet wine of Bordeaux, but it had become a difficult sell—not many consumers were interested in dessert wines. So Sauternes producers decided to try to reposition Sauternes as a food wine, specifically a wine that could go well with spicy Asian dishes. But the problem with this lunch was that it was held at a restaurant that made no concessions to delicate Western palates. The food was very spicy, and the spiciness overwhelmed the wines. It overwhelmed one of the winemakers, too: as she was extolling the wonders of Sauternes and Indian cuisine, I noticed that beads of sweat were starting to trickle down her face. I toyed with the idea of coming to her rescue with a cold beer, but figured that under the circumstances the gesture probably would not have been appreciated. So she spent the rest of the meal trying, with no success, to douse the fire in her mouth with Sauternes.

"Goes well with Asian cuisine" has lately become a battle cry among vintners who produce wines that have a certain degree of sweetness to them. Off-dry German and Alsatian Rieslings, Sauternes, Port—all of these have been touted as the perfect arm candy for Asian dishes. What's amusing about this meme is that the winemakers and their trade organizations talk about "Asian cuisine" as if there is one common cuisine for the whole of Asia, from Karachi to Kyoto. That is obviously not the case, and some Asian cuisines are wine-friendlier than others. I think wine does very nicely with Japanese fare. Champagne, white Burgundies, and dry white Loire Valley wines are great with sushi, and they match well with Japanese preparations generally. Chinese cooking, too, lends itself well to wine, the exception being fiery Sichuan cuisine. Those same Champagnes, white Burgundies, and Loire whites also do well with most Chinese food; with meat, pork, and poultry dishes, you can go with a red wine—preferably something on the lighter side, with good acidity.

But with other Asian cuisines, wine can be a real challenge. Authentic Thai food is very hot, for instance, and can completely dull the flavors of a delicate German Riesling. The same is true of Vietnamese and Indian cuisine. If the spiciness is toned down, the wine can perhaps stand up to the food, but if not, the wine can too easily become a casualty of the meal. It might be heresy for a wine writer to say this, but I think beer is usually the best option with these cuisines, and that is unquestionably true of another Asian cuisine, Korean. I happen to adore Korean food and have learned through hard experience that Korean cuisine and wine don't mix. I don't even try to mix them anymore; I just order beer to go with the bulgogi. Many of us are eating a lot of Asian food these days—it is more readily available than ever before, and it is delicious. But don't let all this chatter about how gloriously certain wines match with Asian cuisines deceive you. Some Asian cuisines lend themselves to wine drinking, and others emphatically do not.

# 6

---

# Back to the Future
# in California

I T  I S  P O S S I B L Y the most famous wine story ever, but on the chance that you are one of the three people who hasn't heard it, let me recap it. On May 24, 1976, a blind tasting pitting some illustrious French wines against a group of unknown California reds and whites took place at the Intercontinental Hotel in Paris. The event was organized by Steve Spurrier, a dandyish Brit who owned a wine shop and wine school in Paris. It was America's Bicentennial year, Spurrier had been impressed by the wines that he'd tasted on a recent visit to California, and he thought it would be fun and enlightening to assemble a group of French wine eminences for a comparative tasting. Little did he expect that they would choose the 1973 Stag's Leap Cabernet Sauvignon and the 1973 Chateau Montelena Chardonnay as their top wines, besting the likes of Haut-Brion and Mouton Rothschild. The United States beats France at wine! The Judgment of Paris, as the tasting came to be known, made headlines around the world and heralded in the most dramatic way imaginable California's emergence as a wine region. Far from being a viticultural backwater, Napa turned out wines that could go toe-to-toe with the finest wines that France had to offer.

In the aftermath of the Paris tasting, some French winemakers wisely recognized that France could no longer take its viticultural supremacy for granted, and they responded by improving the quality of their wines. Aubert de Villaine, the coproprietor of Burgundy's Domaine de la Romanée-Conti, had been one of the judges in Paris, and although he was briefly persona non grata after returning home, he said that the result of the tasting had been a great "kick in the ass" for French winemaking. As for American winemaking, the result was, not surprisingly, cause for euphoria, and it was also a source of motivation: it was affirmation that California could indeed make truly great wines, and it spurred other vintners to seek to maximize the quality of their reds and whites.

Indeed, it quickly became an article of faith that California had one enormous, possibly decisive advantage over France: it had a reliably warm, sunny climate, and France did not. Winemakers in Burgundy and Bordeaux were lucky if they got two or three good vintages a decade. In California, by contrast, it was a rare decade that didn't cough up eight or nine good vintages. It seemed that the future belonged to California, and for a long time California lived up to the lofty expectations. Some sensational wines were produced there during the late 1970s and through the 1980s.

But in the early to mid-1990s, something went wrong. In my opinion, the last truly great vintage for California was 1991, which yielded a bumper crop of brilliant wines—Ridge Monte Bello, Dominus, Montelena Estate, Phelps Insignia, Spottswoode,

Mondavi Reserve. These were sun-splashed but elegant wines, equal parts power and finesse. In subsequent vintages, however, the power began to eclipse the finesse. Alcohol levels shot up, as did the influence of new oak. It probably began with the 1994 vintage, was unmistakable in the 1997 vintage, and became the defining attribute of higher-end California wines by the early 2000s. What drove the trend is the subject of spirited debate. Some attribute it to climate change; others claim that it was due to winemakers' catering to Robert Parker's taste for hedonistic fruit bombs. But I think that the original sin was believing that sun mattered more than soil. California wines may have triumphed in the Judgment of Paris, but centuries of trial and error had taught the French two critically important lessons: it is essential to match the right grapes to the right sites, and the most interesting wines don't merely taste good, they reflect the particular attributes of the vineyards from which they emerge. Only now, forty years after the Judgment of Paris, has California come to the realization that *terroir* matters above all else, and as a result, a truly golden age of California winemaking may be at hand.

This is not to suggest that no one in California grasped the importance of *terroir* a generation ago. Paul Draper at Ridge Vineyards, arguably California's greatest winery, certainly understood that site selection was critical to making distinctive, compelling wines. Ridge's Monte Bello vineyard, located high in the Santa Cruz Mountains, where Ridge produces its benchmark Cabernet Sauvignon, is one of the world's great *terroirs*. Ditto the Geyserville vineyard in Sonoma County, which produces Ridge's completely sui generis Geyserville Zinfandel. Josh Jensen, a Yale graduate who became convinced that limestone-rich soil was the key to Burgundy's success with Pinot and Chardonnay, established a winery on the site of a former limestone quarry in the

## THE SANTA CRUZ MOUNTAINS:
### CALIFORNIA'S REAL SWEET SPOT?

The Judgment of Paris elevated the stature of California wines; more than that, it catapulted Napa Valley to stardom. Foreign oenophiles flocked to Napa to see the vineyards and taste the wines. It quickly became received wisdom that Napa was America's viticultural heartland, the source of our finest wines. In time Sonoma acquired considerable cachet of its own, and later, thanks in no small part to *Sideways*, the Central Coast was heralded as the third leg of this stool, the third of California's three great wine regions. But while Napa, Sonoma, and the Central Coast are capable of turning out fantastic wines, the Santa Cruz range south of San Francisco has proven itself over the years to be California's true sweet spot. Rhys Vineyards is writing just the latest chapter in this often-overlooked region's illustrious winemaking history, a history that dates back to the late nineteenth century and that includes such iconic names as Martin Ray and Paul Masson.

What's so impressive about the Santa Cruz range is not just the quality of the wines it produces but the variety. This fairly compact area has shown itself capable of turning out brilliant Cabernets, Chardonnays, Pinot Noirs, and Syrahs. The mere fact that it has had so much success with Cabernet and Pinot Noir, grapes that generally flourish under very different circumstances and that yield polar-opposite wines, speaks to the unrivaled versatility of the San Francisco peninsula. And while this is just one man's opinion, I can say that the finest California Cabernets, Pinots, Syrahs, and Chardonnays that I've tasted have all come from the

Santa Cruz range. The wines of Ridge, Mount Eden, and now Rhys are benchmarks as far as California goes—yardsticks against which all other wines must be measured. The fact that some of the brightest stars from other parts of California, such as Pax Mahle and the team of Duncan Arnot Meyers and Nathan Lee Roberts, are now making wines in the Santa Cruz range speaks to the quality that this area is capable of turning out. It is not an easy place to make wines; it is very rugged, and crop yields tend to be pretty meager. Because the output is so relatively puny, the Santa Cruz range will surely never have the kind of broad recognition and appeal that Napa, Sonoma, and the Central Coast enjoy. Nor is it ever likely to be a tourist mecca, though its spectacular scenery and proximity to both Silicon Valley and San Francisco make it a natural attraction. However, based on past and present performance, a strong case can be made that the Santa Cruz range is the source of California's most compelling wines, and given the intrinsic quality of the area's vineyards, the future promises to be just as lustrous.

remote Galivan Mountains near Monterey back in the 1970s. Calera Wine Company, as it is known, has been producing some of California's finest, most expressive wines ever since. Moreover, several California vineyards have also demonstrated the ability to yield brilliant wines via multiple producers, which is one test of great *terroir*. For instance, a half-dozen different producers, dating back to the early 1970s and including names like Ridge and Joseph Phelps, have made sensational Cabernets using fruit harvested from Napa's Eisele Vineyard. The Eisele property is as good an example as one could hope to find of the importance of *terroir*, but it is only belatedly that *terroir* has become a mantra among California producers.

For most of the past two decades, a lot of vines were planted in California not because they were necessarily compatible with the vineyards but simply because they were fashionable grapes. Pinot Noir is hot—let's plant some Pinot here! Even at the highest end, proper site selection was often treated as a secondary concern. Fueled by the tech boom, a number of newly enriched tycoons started wineries in Napa in the 1990s. Their aim was to produce boutique wines that would garner high scores from Parker and the *Wine Spectator* and become trophies for other rich people, and they all seemed to think that hiring big-name consulting winemakers—Helen Turley, Michel Rolland, Heidi Barrett—ultimately mattered more than their choice of vineyards. For the purpose of achieving ecstatic reviews from Parker and the *Spectator*, that seems to have been true.

However, a lot of those wines have lost their cachet in recent years. Part of it is the economic downturn—consumers are no longer quite so willing to drop $150 or $200 (or more) on a bottle of Napa Cabernet—but I have to believe that part of it is also that many of these wines just weren't very interesting. They all had the same basic taste profile: overripe fruit, lots of new oak, and little, if any, obvious site expression. These wines provoked a strong backlash in the geekier precincts of the wine world; indeed, California became every wine geek's favorite punching bag. Denouncing California wines as overripe, overoaked, overwrought, and overpriced was commonplace in these circles. In fact, scorning California was considered a mark of sophistication, a measure of one's wine savviness. The scorn wasn't unjustified: many higher-end California wines were oafish confections.

But recent years have also seen the emergence of a group

of winemakers who are fixated on the notion of *terroir* and who are determined to put a different face on California wines—to show that California can produce balanced, elegant, subtle wines. With Burgundy rather than Bordeaux as their beacon, they have been seeking out cool-climate sites in which to plant Pinot Noir and Chardonnay (as well as some other grape varieties, notably Syrah), and the results have been hugely impressive. These are some of the most exciting wines to emerge from California, and they suggest that after a two-decades-long detour, California is back on track to realizing the promise that the Judgment of Paris hinted at.

So who are the winemakers at the vanguard of this movement? They include a former Wall Streeter turned Pinot Noir specialist named Jamie Kutch, the San Francisco sommelier Rajat Parr, and a Silicon Valley entrepreneur named Kevin Harvey. All three honed their palates on Burgundies and set out to make wines that showed the same finesse and site expression of Burgundies. Others followed a more twisted path. Take Wells Guthrie, a Los Angeles native in his early forties. In 2000, Guthrie launched a Sonoma-based winery called Copain. His lush, high-alcohol Pinot Noirs and Syrahs quickly earned stellar ratings from Parker and other critics and a loyal following among consumers. There was just one problem: Guthrie wasn't all that jazzed about his own wines. They didn't have the freshness he wanted—fruit with some crunch to it—and he found that they grew soft and flabby as they aged. Also, because of the alcohol and density, they weren't great with food. Guthrie had trained in the northern Rhône Valley and had also tasted his share of great Burgundies, and he wanted his wines to have some of that Old World nuance. At no small risk to his business, he decided to take his wines in another direction. He began focusing on cooler vineyards and went north of Sonoma, to Mendocino County, to find sites that could yield the kind of restrained, graceful Pinots, Syrahs, and Chardonnays that he hoped to make. He also started picking grapes earlier to keep the alcohol levels in check and to lock in the freshness that he sought. Some fans weren't pleased with the slimmed-down Copain, but Guthrie was much happier with the wines, and the market has now come around to his point of view; the wines have been enthusiastically embraced by sommeliers on both coasts and by many consumers, too.

For my taste, the most thrilling of the newer wines are coming from Kevin Harvey, whose winery, Rhys Vineyards, is located in the Santa Cruz Mountains. Rhys is a classic case of one man's obsession run splendidly amok. Harvey, a tall, genial Silicon Valley software entrepreneur, caught the wine bug in the early 1990s. It soon mutated into a Burgundy fixation, and in 1995 he decided to dabble in fantasy by planting some Pinot Noir vines— Burgundy's signature red grape variety— in the backyard of his Woodside, California, home, set in the foothills of the Santa Cruz range. He vinified the grapes in his garage, and the wine turned out to be shockingly good. (He insists that he had no clue his lawn could cough up such quality; he says it was "pure serendipity.") He had been thinking about starting a winery in Sonoma, but it now occurred to him that there might be gold in the mountains behind his house.

Further exploration—and Harvey was nothing if not diligent—revealed that the steep inclines of the Santa Cruz Mountains were carpeted with rocks and also had very shallow, weathered soils. From his travels, Harvey had observed that many of Europe's most acclaimed vineyards were situated on land just like that. Thin, poor soil is desirable because it forces vines to struggle for nutrients, which has the effect of limiting their output and yielding very concentrated fruit. According to Harvey, it also causes the grapes to ripen relatively early, which keeps alcohol levels in check. As for those rocks, it wasn't just their prevalence that was notable; it was also their variety. The Santa Cruz appellation is bisected by the San Andreas Fault, which is where the North American and Pacific tectonic plates collide, and all that churning has created remarkable geological diversity. The hillsides are strewn with chert, shale, limestone, mudstone, and sandstone. Intuitively, at least, this combination of factors seemed to account for the piercing minerality that Harvey had found in his backyard *cuvée* and other Santa Cruz wines.

He began scouring the region for potential vineyards and between 2001 and 2005 identified and developed four sites to go along with the one behind his house, which he had aptly christened Home Vineyard (there is now a sixth vineyard, located in the Anderson Valley north of Sonoma). The vineyards ranged in elevation from 400 to 2,300 feet and had cool microclimates and very distinct soils. They were farmed biodynamically, and the winemaking regimen, overseen by Jeff Brinkman, was uniform across all the vineyards—mostly whole-cluster fermentations, natural yeasts, limited use of new oak— in the belief that this would isolate and accentuate the soil expression.

The results have been pinch-me brilliant. The Rhys wines are hypnotically good—crisp, poised, succulent, with sensational minerality and structure. Deceptively pale in color, as the best Pinots often are, they are also astonishingly low in alcohol; some of them clock in under 13 percent. What makes the wines even more impressive is that they share all these qualities yet are strikingly different from one another. Harvey's experiment is succeeding. The Rhys wines truly are *vins de terroir*, with an individuality that seems clearly derived from the soil.

Known as the "heartbreak grape," Pinot Noir is a notoriously capricious variety. Burgundy, where it has reigned since the late fourteenth century, seemed to be the only place it was capable of flourishing, and even there it could be maddeningly hit-or-miss. A lot of Pinot has been planted in California, Oregon, and New Zealand, and some good wines have been made. Even so, Burgundy nuts like me were convinced that Pinot was truly at home only in the limestone-rich soils of east-central France and that New World renderings were forever destined to be also-rans. Rhys has cracked the code, however, turning out delicious Pinots that in their subtlety, elegance, and sense of place approach the very best red Burgundies. I think all they lack at this point is the same intensity and length of flavor, which will presumably come with vine age, and a demonstrated ability to gain complexity as they mature, and I am confident that will happen, too.

### Should There Be Formal Classifications for California Wines?

A few years ago, Sea Smoke Cellars, which is located in Santa Barbara County, put the words *California Grand Cru* on the labels of all six of the wines that it made in 2009. It was a pretty bold claim, considering that California doesn't have a formal hierarchy of vineyards or wineries. The fact that Sea Smoke had been in existence for barely a decade, with a vineyard that in its previous incarnation had been a bean field, made it a particularly brash move.

The controversy kicked up by this act of self-aggrandizement raised anew the question of whether California should have an official pecking order—a ranking of wineries *à la* the 1855 Bordeaux classifications, or a ranking of vineyards *à la* the Burgundy *cru* system. My take? No way. For one thing, although wine has been produced in California since the mid-nineteenth century, the state has too short a viticultural history to contemplate that kind of codification. Sure, some California wines are clearly first-growth caliber—the Ridge Monte Bello Cabernet Sauvignon leaps to mind. But the Monte Bello is also an anomaly as California goes, in that it has been an outstanding wine for more than four decades. When two or three dozen California wines have shown that kind of sustained excellence, we can talk about classifying California wineries.

As for categorizing vineyards, that would be seriously misguided at this point. California is still trying to match the right grapes to the right soils and microclimates. With all due respect to Sea Smoke, it is a little premature to be handing out (or appropriating) *grand cru* honors. Many of California's most promising sites are fairly new and have only ever had one owner. The strength of the Burgundian model is that its top vineyards have demonstrated their worthiness over hundreds of years and in the hands of multiple growers. (With rare exception, ownership of vineyards in Burgundy is divided among numerous parties; one producer will own two rows of vines, another will have four, and so on. The twenty-acre Montrachet vineyard, for instance, source of Burgundy's most coveted white wines, currently has eighteen different owners.) There are certainly sites in California that have hinted at that sort of consistency; a number of producers have coaxed great wines out of the aforementioned Eisele Vineyard, for instance. But they are few in number.

Beyond all that, I just think the idea of binding wine classifications is somehow un-American. Whatever its merits, the 1855 ladder in Bordeaux created a viticultural caste system, and the *cru* mechanism had a similar effect in Burgundy. Obviously, a winemaker in Burgundy can improve his lot merely by acquiring land in a great vineyard, whereas in Bordeaux he would have to purchase an entire château. But the point stands. Sure, there are good vineyards, bad vineyards, and great vineyards; the same is true of wineries. Those distinctions exist irrespective of whether they are formally acknowledged. But we Americans don't do caste systems; we are all about upward mobility (or at least we used to be), and establishing official rankings strikes me as antithetical to that spirit. And yes, for any classification to be meaningful, it would necessarily have to be unchanging, or at least glacially slow to change. If the rankings were constantly being shuffled, they would quickly lose their credibility.

Also, the problems of the appellation system in France these days ought to serve as a cautionary tale. The Appellations d'Origine Contrôlée (AOC for short) system was established in 1935. The goal was to map out the boundaries in which certain wines, such as Hermitage, could be made, and to prevent those names from being used elsewhere. But the AOC setup was also meant to serve as a quality control mechanism: AOC status was supposed to be granted only to France's finest vineyards and, by extension, its finest wines.

However, starting in the 1970s, largely in response to political pressure—winemakers whose vineyards were not AOC-designated pushed to be included because they wanted to be able to claim greater prestige for their wines and charge higher prices for them—the number of appellations exploded. These days, more than 50 percent of France's vineyards enjoy AOC status. This has seriously undermined the credibility of the appellation system, as has the way that appellations are governed. Individual wine appellations are basically administered by the winemakers themselves, and this arrangement, plainly fraught with conflicts of interest, has had terrible consequences. In numerous appellations, the mediocre majority rules, and quality has consequently suffered. For a wine to be labeled AOC, for instance, it must pass a taste test, but in many appellations the taste test is a joke—almost every wine gets waved through.

Even crazier, though, is what has happened in places like the Loire Valley and Beaujolais, where some of the finest producers—Jean-Paul Brun, Jean Thévenet, Marcel Richaud—have had their wines rejected. While it can't be proven, it is widely assumed that these winemakers have been targeted by neighbors jealous of their success—a wine version of Gulliver and the Lilliputians. These are areas in which many vintners are struggling economically, and there is resentment of those who are prospering, resentment that appears to have found expression in the form of failed taste tests. I'm not suggesting that the codification of California wines would necessarily result in the same sort of problems that are found in France, but the French example is another reason I think we can get along just fine without having an official hierarchy of vineyards or wineries.

## HOW DID THE FRENCH GET TO BE SO GOOD AT WINE?

Having spent several paragraphs talking about the problems of the French appellation system, let me now shower some praise on the French. Why, historically, have the French been so good at wine? One reason is that they've been making it a lot longer than the rest of us. But like many oenophiles, I'm convinced that it's also a function of the philosophy that guides their efforts. At the heart of the French viticultural system is the concept of *terroir*: the idea that wine is chiefly a product of the physical environment (the soil, the microclimate) in which the grapes are grown, that matching the right grape to the right soil is the essential first step to making fine wine, and that a wine should not just taste good but exude a sense of place. This notion took root in France during the Middle Ages and remains the organizing principle of French winemaking. But many New World producers, explicitly and implicitly, have shown contempt for it. They have allowed commercial considerations to dictate which grapes they plant, paying little regard to whether those grapes are really suited to the sites in question, and they have demonstrated a proclivity to make wines that emphasize fruit, alcohol, and new oak over any expression of *terroir*. Their wines exude an unmistakable sense of place, but it's the wrong place—the cellar rather than the vineyard.

Not surprisingly, these wines often seem indistinguishable from one another, and I think this sameness goes a long way to explaining why so many oenophiles are ultimately drawn to France. *Terroir* is a somewhat elusive concept, and the extent to which the vineyard really influences the taste of a wine is something we may never know. But the finest vintners in places such as Burgundy and the Loire continue to produce wines that convey a sense of "somewhereness," to use Matt Kramer's felicitous phrase, and that on balance show more nuance and individuality than most of what emerges from Napa or Barossa. When it comes to crafting interesting, multidimensional wines that will improve with age, France still leads the way. But California has exceptional *terroir*, too, and with the advent of this movement toward greater balance and site expression, it is slowly catching up. I think we are on the cusp of a very special era for California winemaking, a truly great leap forward, and as big a blow as the Judgment of Paris was for the French, it was nothing compared to what's probably coming.

## THE NEW CALIFORNIA— NAMES WORTH KNOWING

- Rhys Vineyards (Pinot Noir, Chardonnay, Syrah)
- Copain Wines (Pinot Noir, Chardonnay, Syrah)
- Wind Gap Wines (Syrah, Pinot Noir, Chardonnay)
- Dashe Cellars (Zinfandel, Riesling)
- Lioco Winery (Pinot Noir, Chardonnay, blends)
- Sandhi Wines (Pinot Noir, Chardonnay)
- Tyler Winery (Pinot Noir, Chardonnay)
- Kutch Wines (Pinot Noir)
- Arnot-Roberts (Syrah, Pinot Noir, Cabernet Sauvignon, Chardonnay)
- Donkey and Goat Winery (Syrah, Grenache, Grenache Blanc, Chardonnay, blends)
- Failla Wines (Pinot Noir, Chardonnay, Syrah)

## THE BEST OF CALIFORNIA'S OLD GUARD

- Ridge Vineyards (Cabernet Sauvignon, Chardonnay, Zinfandel)
- Chateau Montelena (Cabernet Sauvignon, Chardonnay, Riesling, Zinfandel)
- Mayacamas Vineyards (Cabernet Sauvignon, Chardonnay)
- Dominus (Cabernet Sauvignon)
- Stony Hill Vineyard (Chardonnay)

- Nalle Winery (Zinfandel)
- Smith-Madrone Vineyards (Cabernet Sauvignon, Chardonnay, Riesling)
- Hanzell Vineyards (Chardonnay)
- Au Bon Climat Winery (Pinot Noir, Chardonnay)
- Calera Wine (Pinot Noir, Chardonnay)

⊶⊷

# 7

# The Beaune Supremacy:
# The Triumph of Burgundy

*L*OOKING FOR a quick means of establishing your wine-geek bona fides? Here's one easy and surefire way: declare your passion for Burgundy and simultaneously announce that you have sworn off Bordeaux, and you will instantaneously acquire all the street cred you could possibly want. Burgundy ascendant, Bordeaux passé? Yep, and it's arguably the biggest wine story of the past decade. For the better part of two centuries, Bordeaux was the most important and influential wine region and source of the most coveted wines. Now, though, its longtime rival to the north, Burgundy, has largely supplanted Bordeaux as the wine world's lodestar. What accounts for this historic change? I think it speaks to a growing preference for Pinot Noir, Burgundy's red grape, over Cabernet Sauvignon, which is Bordeaux's mainstay. But more than that, I believe it reflects a certain romanticism on the part of wine enthusiasts—

a preference for the artisanal over the industrial, an emotional disposition that small is indeed beautiful.

Burgundy is a relatively tiny region located in east-central France. Almost all its wines are made from a single grape— Pinot Noir for the reds, Chardonnay for the whites (there is another white grape, Aligoté, but it is made in minute quantities). Bordeaux, located in southwestern France, specializes in blended wines. Bordeaux is divided into two parts, known as the left bank and the right bank (they are divided by the Gironde River). Cabernet Sauvignon is king on the left bank, Merlot on the right, but neither grape is used exclusively. A typical left bank wine is a blend of Cabernet Sauvignon and Merlot, with Cabernet Franc and Petit Verdot possibly thrown in. A typical right bank wine is predominately Merlot, with Cabernet Franc and possibly also Cabernet Sauvignon added. In Burgundy, the vineyard is king; the region's wines are classified by vineyard (*grand cru, premier cru, villages*, and so on), and a winery's standing is wholly dependent on the vineyards that it owns. In Bordeaux, by contrast, the château is king; wines are classified by château (first growth, second growth, and the like), and if Château Lafite, a first growth, acquires a vineyard that previously belonged to a third growth, that vineyard will, by dint of association, suddenly be producing first-growth fruit.

Burgundy has always had its loyalists, of course, and they've tended to be fanatically partisan. Indeed, among a small, well-heeled segment of the wine-drinking public, Burgundy has long enjoyed cultish devotion; like surfers roaming the globe in search of the perfect wave, Burgundy devotees spend countless hours and jaw-dropping amounts of cash chasing the elusive, infatuating "Burgundy high." While usually not obnoxious about it, these Burgundy aficionados believe that they possess particularly refined palates and have found a "higher truth" in wine.

And just as there are Burg fanatics, so there are equally impassioned Burg-phobes. These are drinkers who have no patience for Burgundy's Byzantine complexity and who find the wines too light, too dainty for their taste. They generally view the Burgundy crowd as masochists and cranks. The leading Burgundy basher has always been Robert Parker. Over the years he has lavished high scores on many Burgundies, but they are not his preferred style, and he was never Burgundy's preferred critic. Indeed, he eventually became persona non grata there and had to hire an assistant to cover the region. The experience left him nursing a grudge: he seems to go out of his way to bait the Burgundy faithful. If a Burgundy vintage falls short in his view, he tends to dismiss it in sweeping, contemptuous terms, something he almost never does with feebler years in, say, Bordeaux or the Rhône.

But when it comes to Burgundy—and this is perhaps the most telling sign of his waning influence—Parker is spitting into the wind these days. That's because Burgundy has lately become the touchstone for many wine enthusiasts. It is often said in wine circles that all roads lead to Burgundy, and never has that been truer than now, when more and more wine enthusiasts seem to be falling under Burgundy's spell. One reason is the growing popularity of Pinot Noir. While fine Pinots are being produced in California, Oregon, and New Zealand, the finest ones still come from Burgundy, and it is fair to say that once turned on to the pleasures of Chambolle-Musigny and Volnay, most Pinot enthusiasts never turn back. And there are a lot of Pinot enthusiasts these days. In 1986 the acclaimed British wine writer Jancis Robinson published a book called *Vines, Grapes, and Wines* in which she observed that "to the great majority of conscious wine-drinking palates in the world today, top quality red wine is Cabernet Sauvignon." I don't think she could make the same claim today, or at least such an unequivocal one. Even before the Great Recession, many American collectors were turning away from Bordeaux and Napa and embracing Burgundy, a development that was part of the broader Pinot Noir boom—a boom that has endured even through the downturn. Does anyone care these days if some hot new Cabernet project is launched in Napa? Not as far as I can tell. An exciting new source of Pinot, however, is sure to generate buzz. For many consumers, Pinot, and especially Pinot in its Burgundian incarnation, is now the gold standard of red wine grapes, and this is surely one big reason that Burgundy has eclipsed Bordeaux.

But Burgundy wouldn't be basking in so much affection these days were it not for the fact that the region has been in the throes of a quality revolution over the past two decades. Parker's attitude toward Burgundy was formed in the 1970s and '80s (and one could argue that it has remained firmly anchored in the past); back then, the quality was spotty, and you'd have to wade through a number of thin, acidic, ungenerous wines to get to that one gem. That is emphatically no longer the case; sensational wines are literally falling off the vines these days in Burgundy.

One reason for the turn in fortune is the improved weather. Climate change poses a long-term threat to Burgundy, but for now it is a boon. In the past twenty years, there has really been only one truly bad vintage, 1994. Every other year has produced at least good wines, and a number of years—1996, 1999, 2001, 2002, 2005, 2009, 2010—have yielded outstanding ones. But the weather is just one factor; better farming is another. The best producers in Burgundy these days—and there are a number of superb ones—are fanatically meticulous farmers. The axiom that great wines are made in the vineyard, not the cellar? Those are truly the words that Burgundy now lives by, and the combination of high-quality fruit and skilled winemaking is yielding consistently excellent wines. It is truly a golden age of Burgundian winemaking, and this is another reason so many people are gravitating toward Burgundy.

But there's a third reason, too, and I think it goes some way to explaining why Burgundy has eclipsed Bordeaux in the hearts and minds of so many: the cultural differences between Burgundy and Bordeaux. Burgundy, with its unpretentious farming culture, represents what we want wine to be; Bordeaux, ever more corporatized and commodified, represents what we don't want it to become. True, Bordeaux has always been the most commercial of wine regions, with a brisk international trade in its wines for centuries. However, the commercialism has been ratcheted up dramatically in recent years. Lots of modest family-run wineries exist on the periphery of Bordeaux, but the limelight belongs to the big-name châteaus. The global wealth boom of the 1990s and early 2000s helped send demand and prices for the most sought-after wines spiraling and also brought an influx of new investors. In his aptly titled book *What Price Bordeaux?*, Benjamin Lewin notes that over the past two decades, wealthy industrialists and big companies have been the fastest-growing category of château owner and today account for roughly one-third of all the classified growths. Lewin says these individuals and entities generally view wine less as a beverage than as a brand, less a source of pleasure than a source of revenue or long-term capital gains.

Burgundy has always been a world apart from Bordeaux. While the Bordelais classified their wines by price, the Burgundians did it on the basis of *terroir*—on what they believed to be the intrinsic quality of each vineyard, as revealed over the centuries. Burgundy's *grand cru* and *premier cru* designations, which were formally introduced in the 1930s, are aesthetic judgments, not commercial benchmarks. Bordeaux has historically been quite affluent and cosmopolitan, a magnet for rich outsiders, foreigners as well as people from other parts of France. In Burgundy, prosperity is a recent phenomenon; up until the 1980s, it was a fairly hardscrabble place (which could explain the lack of rapacious pricing: growers who remember the lean times would rather forgo a few extra euros than risk losing customers—a depression mentality, you could say). It has traditionally been a very insular one, too, composed almost entirely of small, multigenerational family farms. In his book *Bordeaux/Burgundy: A Vintage Rivalry*, Jean-Robert Pitte nicely summarized the atmospheric distinctions:

> Exaggerating only slightly, it is fair to say that in Bordeaux they have university degrees, speak English (and sometimes another foreign language), read the daily financial news, travel frequently to Paris and abroad, dress in the style of English gentlemen farmers, and play tennis or even polo; in short, their manners are sophisticated. Most of their counterparts in Burgundy, by contrast, have no higher education, dress in a rustic or sporty way, in any case without any concern for fashion or affectation, and proudly display their peasant manners. The former spend their time mainly in the office and rely on employees to do the work of the vineyard and the cellar; the latter, even when they have assistance or hired staff, take pleasure in getting out of the office and rolling up their sleeves.

These differences seem more pronounced of late. While Bordeaux is increasingly corporate, its proprietors further removed than ever from the winemaking process, the overwhelming majority of Burgundian estates are still mom-and-pop operations, and the region's agrarian way of life has become even more entrenched. In fact, over the past forty years or so, Burgundy has moved in the direction of greater artisanship. Up until the early 1970s, more than 90 percent of all Burgundies on the market were *négociant* bottlings. *Négociants* are large merchant houses, such as Louis Jadot and Louis Latour, that buy unfinished wines or grapes from growers throughout Burgundy and bottle the finished products under their own labels (some of them also have vineyards of their own). Some of Burgundy's most venerated names—Romanée-Conti, Rousseau, d'Angerville—started bottling their own wines in the early twentieth century, but they were a very distinct minority. For the overwhelming majority of winemakers and vineyard owners in Burgundy, it made much more sense to sell their grapes or unfinished wines to the *négociants*, as their wines wouldn't have sold for enough money to justify the added costs associated with bottling or the added risk of having to sell their wines directly to consumers. That equation began to change in the early 1970s, and it has now changed completely. While the *négociants* are still around and are actually thriving these days, estate bottling is now the norm among quality producers in Burgundy and is really a prerequisite to being taken seriously as a producer.

## CHAMPAGNE: THE SMALL FRY ASCENDANT

This same phenomenon is playing out in the Champagne region of France, with similar results. The Champagne market has traditionally been dominated by large houses like Moët & Chandon, Taittinger, and Veuve Clicquot. These *grandes marques,* as they are known, are *négociants.* Like the *négociants* of Burgundy, they may own a few vineyards of their own, but for the most part they buy grapes from vineyards throughout the vast Champagne region and use them to make their wines. In general, these are not wines that reflect the particular attributes of the vineyards from which they came; instead, the grapes are blended together to create a Champagne that reflects the so-called house style.

But some vineyard owners in Champagne choose not to sell their grapes; instead they make their own Champagnes, and some of them do a really good job. In recent years, the "grower Champagne" movement has turned the chalky hillsides northeast of Paris into arguably the most dynamic wine region on the planet. Indeed, it is quite literally redefining what Champagne is all about. The grower producers work on a much smaller scale than the majors, often using fruit from one village or even a lone vineyard, and often using just one grape variety (Champagne is customarily a blend of Chardonnay, Pinot Noir, and Pinot Meunier). Their goal is not to produce a "house style" but to turn out Champagnes that bear the imprint of the sites from which they emanated— that have a strong *goût de terroir.*

The growers and *grandes marques* are in a battle of competing visions about what Champagne should be, and the growers are winning. The big producers, despite the fact that they function in exactly the same way that the Burgundy *négociants* do, are now seen as the Champagne equivalent of the major Bordeaux châteaus: soulless corporate entities that regard their own wines not as agricultural products but as luxury brands. The growers, by contrast, are seen as champions of the Burgundy model: plucky artisans crafting authentic, *terroir*-driven wines. And how do we know the growers are winning? For one thing, their Champagnes generate a lot more buzz these days than the big-house bubblies. But even more significant, where the growers have led, the big houses are starting to follow. The *grandes marques* are increasingly experimenting with single-vineyard and single-grape wines, which speaks to just how dramatically the "farmer fizz" phenomenon has transformed Champagne.

Names to know among grower Champagnes:

- Pierre Moncuit
- Egly-Ouriet
- Pierre Peters
- Jacques Selosse
- Vilmart
- Pierre Gimonnet
- Larmandier-Bernier
- Cédric Bouchard
- Ulysse Collin
- Henri Billiot
- Camille Savès
- Jacques Lassaigne
- Gatinois
- Agrapart

So Burgundy has gone in the direction of greater smallness in recent decades. In contrast to Bordeaux, winery owners in Burgundy almost always do the winemaking themselves, and these days the amount of time that a vintner spends in the fields is seen as a measure of his or her commitment to quality. The idea that great wines are made in the vineyard is now Burgundy's mantra, and its best producers work their vines with a fastidiousness that would put their fathers and grandfathers to shame. With Burgundy, you are not drinking a luxury label owned by a guy in a Brioni suit but rather a wine made by a farmer dressed in boots, and for me and many others this authenticity, the sense that the wines are somehow closer to the earth, is also part of Burgundy's attraction relative to Bordeaux.

Above all, I suspect that Burgundy's growing allure and Bordeaux's corresponding decline is a statement about what people value in their glass. The wines we feel most passionate about are those that offer not only compelling aromas and flavors but a little romance and soul, too. It is hard to discern these qualities in most Bordeaux nowadays; however good the wines may taste, they have become so bound up in prices, scores, and luxury marketing that the romance and soul have been drained out of them. For me, and I think for an increasing number of wine drinkers, what appeals about Burgundy is not only the excellence of the wines but the charm and character of the place itself.

## WHAT'S KILLING ALL THE WHITE BURGUNDIES?

Burgundy is not an unambiguous success story. While this may be a golden age for the region's red wines, it is a very different story with the white wines. Beginning with the 1995 vintage, large numbers of white Burgundies have fallen victim to premature oxidation; wines that should still taste young and full of promise are turning up dead in the bottle. They have the color of apple juice, smell like Sherry, and are undrinkable. I have a fairly extensive white Burgundy collection, and almost without fail now, the wines I have from the period 1996 through 2002 are kaput—and 2002 is by no means the last year affected by the "premox" problem. In fact, the problem is so bad that a lot of collectors no longer buy white Burgundies, or they choose to drink them very young in order to mitigate the risk.

It is a huge problem. Worse than that, it has become a scandal. That's because the Burgundians were slow to acknowledge the problem, and a lot of Burgundy enthusiasts in the wine trade have also been reluctant to speak publicly about it. More frustrating, we still don't know what is causing all these wines to suffer premature oxidation. A number of theories have been mooted. One possible culprit is the corks: it has been suggested that hydrogen peroxide, which is used to clean corks, was not properly removed from many stoppers during the period in question, and because hydrogen peroxide is an oxidant, these stoppers may have ended up killing the wines they were meant to protect. Another theory is that producers eased up too much on the use of sulfur dioxide, which serves as an antioxidant, or were doing too much *battonage* (stirring the lees, which imparts greater richness to wines but also exposes them to more oxygen).

Not every producer has been hit by the premox problem. Coche-Dury and Domaine Leflaive, two of the greatest producers of white Burgundies, seem to have avoided it. And bizarrely, many oenophiles report that the incidence of premature oxidation can vary even in the same case of wine: some bottles might be good while others are completely shot. But the bottom line is that a huge number of white Burgundies produced since 1995 have succumbed to premox, and the problem doesn't appear to be going away (people have reported premoxed wines from 2007 and 2008, both highly regarded vintages for white Burgundies). My advice: I wouldn't stop drinking white Burgundies—they offer great pleasure even when really young—but I would make sure to consume them within the first 3–5 years. With all due respect to Orson Welles, this is one instance in which it is best to serve wines before their time.

## DOMAINE DE LA ROMANÉE-CONTI: IS IT REALLY THAT GOOD?

Yes, it is. The wines of Domaine de la Romanée-Conti are prohibitively expensive these days, and for those who enjoy endless, inconclusive debates, there is a spirited one to be had about whether the DRC wines are worth the money. But there is no denying the quality: collectively, the seven DRC *grand cru* reds represent the greatest expressions of Pinot Noir in the world, and the lone white sold by the domaine, the Montrachet, is arguably the finest Chardonnay on the planet. The most sought-after of the reds is the Romanée-Conti, produced from the vineyard of that name, which the domaine solely owns (what is known as a *monopole*). A tiny vineyard—it's just over four acres and yields a mere six thousand bottles annually—Romanée-Conti has been making oenophiles swoon for centuries. A document from the French Revolution described the vineyard as "the most excellent of all those of the Côte d'Or . . . Its brilliant and velvety color, its ardor and scent, charm all the senses . . . Well kept, it always improves as it approaches its eighth or tenth year; it is then a balm for the elderly, the feeble and the disabled, and will restore life to the dying." Who wouldn't pay a fortune for a wine with powers like that? This long-standing reputation for greatness speaks to the quality of the vineyard's *terroir*; there is simply no piece of land yet known to man that draws such quality out of the Pinot Noir grape. A close second is DRC's other *monopole*, the vineyard known as La Tâche; it yields the most seductively perfumed and elegant wine I've ever encountered. The other DRC reds can be pretty spectacular, too, and the Montrachet is amazing. There are lots of sensational Burgundies to choose from, but DRC remains the benchmark—something to keep in mind for when you win the lottery.

## VALUE AND BURGUNDY IN THE SAME SENTENCE?

Yes, there is such a thing as value in Burgundy—relatively speaking. There is no such thing as a $10 Burgundy that's worth drinking. But if you are willing to go up to $20, you can start to find some good wines, particularly from Burgundy's periphery, namely the Côte Chalonnaise and the Mâcon. Some very good stuff is produced in these parts, and the wines are affordable for nonplutocrats. One caveat, however: in my experience, vintage tends to matter more with lower-caste Burgundies than it does with wines from the Côte d'Or, where the greatest vineyards are. In challenging years, the best producers on the Côte d'Or will still manage to turn out plenty of excellent wines. By contrast, "value" Burgundies can be pretty lean and shrill in off years. That's particularly true of the reds. But in warmer, riper years—and 2009 was a great example of this—those same wines can drink exceedingly well.

Another source of value in Burgundy: *négociant* wines. Along with the rest of Burgundy, the *négociants* were in a rut during the 1970s and 1980s. But these days the better ones are thriving as perhaps never before. Louis Jadot, Drouhin, and Bouchard Père et Fils, which are considered the three strongest *négociant* houses at the moment, are all turning out sensational wines, and while their *grands crus* and *premiers crus* can be expensive, they also make stellar village and regional wines that can be had for very reasonable prices. Affordable Burgundy—yes, there is such a thing.

## ARE THE BORDEAUX FIRST GROWTHS REALLY FIRST?

An indispensable rite of passage for any oenophile is to taste one of the five Bordeaux first growths: Château Lafite, Château Latour, Château Mouton Rothschild, Château Margaux, and Château Haut-Brion. Nearly 160 years after the 1855 classifications were drafted, first-growth status remains Bordeaux's ultimate mark of prestige and a powerful marketing tool. Indeed, many people now regard the first growths more as luxury brands than as wines, a view that the châteaus themselves haven't necessarily discouraged (and certainly not with their, shall we say, aggressive pricing). But there has long been a debate about whether these five estates deserve the premium they command. In blind tastings pitting the first growths against lesser Bordeaux, it is often the case that the first growths do not finish on top; in fact, from my purely unscientific observations, that seems to be the norm in tastings involving professionals and amateurs alike. It is no accident that during the annual spring barrel tastings in Bordeaux, the first growths do not allow their wines to be tasted blind—enough poor showings and people might decide that these wines maybe aren't so special. My view on the matter is, well, complicated. On the one hand, I'm an ardent empiricist, and if blind tastings show that the firsts cannot reliably finish first, then one at least has to grant the possibility that the firsts aren't really first.

However, I have had too many amazing experiences with the first growths to conclude that they are overrated, and I've been doing this long enough—tasting wines—that I can honestly say that labels really don't sway me. In fact, the loftier a wine's reputation, the more skepticism I bring to the table (prove that you are good as everyone says!). The first growths are not superior to the grandees of the right bank—Pétrus, Cheval Blanc, Lafleur—but they have demonstrated over many decades a capacity for greatness. The 1945 Haut-Brion, 1961 Latour, 1982 Lafite, 2000 Margaux—if these wines don't make you weak-kneed, maybe wine isn't really your thing. The only one of the first growths that I have any reservations about is Mouton. It was not actually named a first growth in 1855; it was elevated to the top rung in 1973, after years of lobbying and arm-twisting by the château's owner, the colorful, irrepressible Baron Philippe de Rothschild. Mouton has made a handful of epic wines in the past century, but it has also served up a lot of mediocrity. Château La Mission Haut-Brion (located across the street from Haut-Brion and owned by the same family), a wine that was left out of the 1855 rankings but that ought to be a first growth, has hit more high notes than Mouton and has certainly been more consistent. As for the other four first growths, I like them all, but I have a particular fondness for Haut-Brion; I find it the earthiest, most elegant, and most distinctive of the four.

## NAMES TO KNOW IN BURGUNDY

- Domaine de la Romanée-Conti
- Domaine Leroy
- Domaine Dujac
- Domaine Armand Rousseau
- Domaine Fourrier

- Domaine Georges Roumier
- Domaine Mugnier
- Domaine Ponsot
- Domaine Marquis d'Angerville
- Domaine Michel Lafarge
- Domaine de Montille
- Domaine Comtes de Vogüé
- Domaine J.-F. Coche-Dury
- Domaine Guy Roulot
- Domaine des Comtes Lafon
- Domaine Leflaive
- Domaine Pierre-Yves Colin Morey
- Domaine Raveneau (Chablis)
- Domaine Vincent Dauvissat (Chablis)

# 8

# Great White Hopes

IT IS OFTEN SAID that every white wine secretly wishes it were a red. Winemakers who specialize in white wines can turn a little green with red envy. Some years ago I asked Dominique Lafon, the great Burgundian winemaker whose whites are among the finest in the world, what vineyard in Burgundy he most coveted; without a moment's hesitation, he answered "Musigny," a *grand cru* vineyard that yields some of Burgundy's most enthralling red wines. In addition to his glorious white wines, Lafon made excellent reds from Burgundy's Volnay appellation. However, the wistful look in his eye as he said the word *Musigny* suggested a certain regret at the hand that fate had dealt him: being a master of white wines in a world in which red wines are king. And they are king. At almost any dinner involving both white and red wines, the whites precede the reds; however good the whites might be, they are forever relegated to being the warm-up act, the prelude to the main course.

In contrast to red wines, white wines suffer from what might be called a crisis of authority. With red wines, there is a clear hierarchy: Cabernet Sauvignon is at the top, Pinot Noir is one rung down (but fast gaining on Cabernet), then come Merlot, Syrah, and Grenache, followed by all the rest. While Cabernet and Pinot have their detractors, their continued preeminence is pretty much assured. Things are more fluid (forgive the pun) with white wines. The two most prevalent grapes are Chardonnay and Sauvignon Blanc, but they draw as much flak as they do praise. In the case of Sauvignon Blanc, the ubiquity is completely misleading. Even oenophiles who profess to like Sauvignon Blanc concede that it does not yield particularly profound wines, and more than a few seasoned drinkers despise it.

Possibly the most controversial piece I ever wrote for *Slate* was a column I did in 2006 in which I confessed my hatred of Sauvignon Blanc. "The grape is a dud," I wrote,

> producing chirpy little wines wholly devoid of complexity and depth, the very qualities that make wine interesting and worth savoring . . . Character and verve are two qualities most [Sauvignon Blancs] sorely lack. Sure, they tend to have distinctive bouquets, with heady aromas of grass, citrus, gooseberry, gunflint, and chalk—or some combination thereof. But the excitement is reserved for the nose; all the mouth gets is a limp, lemony liquid that grows progressively more boring with each sip. Sauvignon Blancs almost never evolve in the glass—they simply fill the space . . . Even a simple quaffer ought to be able to hold your interest for at least a few minutes. Sadly, most Sauvignon Blancs can't even do that. In fact, the pleasure to be derived from the typical Sauvignon Blanc is inversely related to the amount of attention paid to the wine—the less you think about it, the more you're apt to enjoy it. And spare me that old chestnut about versatility: it is

hardly surprising, given their acute lack of personality, that these smiley-face wines can accommodate themselves to just about any dish. Water can, too.

Not surprisingly, the article elicited howls of outrage (though a number of readers expressed agreement), and it remains a sore point with some people even now, years later. All in all, it was a very successful rant. But then, it came from the heart: I really do despise Sauvignon Blanc. In fact, in the years since the *Slate* piece was published, I have periodically purchased Sauvignon Blancs to test if my feelings about the grape were softening or if perhaps I exaggerated how much I disliked it. I can truly say that time has done nothing to dull my hostility toward Sauvignon Blanc. I still consider it a complete dud of a grape. And if you disagree with me? Well, just think of it this way: more for you.

Although Chardonnay is the benchmark among white varietals, it generates almost as much antagonism as Sauvignon Blanc; indeed, it has even inspired a deeply unflattering abbreviation, ABC (anything but Chardonnay). Chardonnay hasn't suffered a backlash like Merlot, but its position is shaky. Like Pinot Noir, Chardonnay reaches its apogee in Burgundy, and although the premature oxidation problem has given white Burgundies a bad name, no one would deny that Burgundy is capable of making wondrous Chardonnays. The same is true of the Champagne region to the north, where some of the greatest wines are *blanc de blancs* (all-Chardonnay bubblies). So what made Chardonnay an object of derision for so many wine enthusiasts? In two words, California Chardonnay. That phrase has almost become a punch line in wine circles; just say "California Chardonnay" in the company of some wine sophisticates and watch as the snickering begins. But the snickering is justified: a lot of really bad Chardonnay is produced in California, including quite a bit of really expensive bad Chardonnay.

During the 1970s consumer interest in Chardonnay began to blossom and the California wine industry started devoting more space to it. In 1972, Jim Barrett, an oenophilic attorney from Southern California, bought Chateau Montelena, which hadn't produced wine commercially since Prohibition, with the intention of turning out Cabernets to rival the best of Bordeaux. Barrett and his winemaker, Mike Grgich, decided to make Chardonnay simply as a way of generating some income while they waited for their newly planted Cabernet vines to bear sufficient fruit. But their Chardonnay did more than just generate some extra cash flow. Astonishingly, the 1973 Montelena Chardonnay, their second vintage, was the winning white wine in the 1976 Judgment of Paris, beating out a handful of famous white Burgundies. Barrett, however, insisted that the Paris result came as no surprise to him. "We've known for a long time that we could put our white Burgundies against anybody's in the world and not take a back seat," he told George Taber of *Time* magazine after the tasting.

California didn't actually make white Burgundies, of course— only Burgundy made white Burgundies. But Barrett's comment spoke to a larger truth: for most of those early Chardonnay producers, the goal was to craft wines in the Burgundian mold. One means to that end was to use French oak barrels to age the wines. James Zellerbach of Sonoma's Hanzell Vineyards, was the pioneering figure on this front; he imported small barrels of Limousin oak, purchased from one of the top coopers in Burgundy, for his Chardonnays. Employed judiciously, oak aging imparts greater complexity to wines, and although Zellerbach's neighbors were apparently dubious, the results he achieved were so impressive that the practice quickly caught on. The 1973 Montelena spent eight months maturing in French barrels before being bottled.

Burgundy remained the inspiration even after the Judgment of Paris, and as Chardonnay's toehold in California turned into a foothold, many newer producers, determined to adhere faithfully to the Burgundian playbook, began putting their wines through malolactic fermentation, a process that converts tart malic acid (at this point, it is customary to say, "Think green apple," so I'll say it: Think green apple) into softer, more palate-friendly lactic acid. It is a necessary step in Burgundy, where the northerly climate can leave the grapes with too much acidic bite. California, though, has the opposite problem: because the weather is often so warm, the grapes can be short on acidity.

Although some of the first serious Chardonnays in California benefited from malolactic fermentation, the process became a standard feature of Chardonnay production in California in the 1980s and frequently yielded thick, creamy, almost zaftig wines that also displayed a pronounced buttery note (a by-product of this secondary fermentation). It didn't help that a lot of vintners were harvesting overripe fruit that was notably deficient in acidity. At the same time, the use of oak turned increasingly indiscriminate, to the point where the wood tended to overwhelm the wine. Thus the irony: classic Burgundian methods ended up taking California Chardonnay in a distinctly un-Burgundian direction. And this was true across all price points, from discount bottlings to high-end ones. Sweet, fat, and oaky emerged as the signature California style.

It is an undeniably popular one, a point underscored by the fact that the amount of California Chardonnay sold annually has quintupled over the last two decades. But you won't find much

California Chardonnay in my cellar. For me, most California Chardonnays are clumsy and cloying; they taste like melted popsicles and are exhausting to drink and pretty much impossible to pair with food. They are often described as cocktail wines, and that's precisely what they are—except I wouldn't want to drink them for cocktails, either. Nor am I a solitary refusenik; lots of grape nuts now live by that aforementioned abbreviation, ABC.

However, some of the long-established names still make svelte, delicious Chardonnays. The list includes not only Montelena and Hanzell but also Ridge Vineyards, Mount Eden, Stony Hill Winery, Mayacamas Vineyards, and Au Bon Climat. And some of the new names mentioned in the California chapter are making sensational Chardonnays in a restrained, Burgundian style, as well. That list includes Rhys, Copain, Wind Gap, Arnot-Roberts, Tyler, and Sandhi (in particular, look for the Rhys Horseshoe Vineyard Chardonnay and the Sandhi Sanford & Benedict Vineyard Chardonnay). But these producers account for just a small fraction of the Chardonnay that is made in California, so how much of a bellwether they are is hard to say. From what I can see, the butterball style of Chardonnay is still quite popular with many vintners and consumers alike; I certainly don't see any indication that these confections are yet going the way of bell-bottoms.

If there is a grape that most wine geeks would like to see eclipse Chardonnay, it is unquestionably Riesling. No grape breeds devotion quite like Reisling, and Riesling has become the darling of sommeliers everywhere. In fact, one of them, the New York sommelier Paul Grieco, is such a Riesling fanatic that he often sports a temporary tattoo with the word *Riesling* in big letters down the length of his right forearm. He also started an annual celebration called the Summer of Riesling. Each summer, restaurants around the United States showcase this Germanic grape in all its geographic and stylistic splendor (Riesling excels at capturing the attributes of the vineyards in which it is grown; it has the same transparency that you find in Pinot Noir). It has been a wildly successful venture that underscores just how popular Riesling has become. In fact, if there is one commandment that holds sway in the wine world today, it is this: thou shalt never speak ill of Riesling.

But Riesling, too, has its problems—specifically, it has an identity problem. Should it be sweet or dry? In France's Alsace region, where Riesling is the primary grape, vintners have split the difference: some of the Rieslings are dry, others are fairly sweet. It is a confusing situation made more confusing by the fact that the labels don't tell you whether the wines are dry or sweet. Essentially, you need to be familiar with the producer's style to know what kind of Riesling you are getting, which is not a great situation for consumers. The most reliably dry Alsatian Rieslings, and the best Alsatian Rieslings I know, come from Trimbach, a venerable producer whose winemaking history dates back to the seventeenth century. Trimbach has two wines, the Cuvée Frédéric Emile and the exceedingly rare Clos Ste. Hune, which I think are two of the finest dry Rieslings on the planet.

But Riesling's true heartland is just over the border from Alsace, in Germany, and for at least the past sixty years or so, a certain amount of sweetness has been a defining attribute of German Rieslings. There is some dispute as to whether the "fruity" style can be described as traditional; while sweet wines enjoyed great prestige in the eighteenth and nineteenth centuries, they were rarities then, and most German wines were apparently fairly dry. The advent of sterile filtration enabled German winemakers to stop fermentations in order to consistently produce wines with discernible amounts of residual sugar. And German consumers developed a raging thirst for such Rieslings after World War II, a fact that is generally attributed to postwar sugar rationing, which had the paradoxical effect of giving Germans an insatiable sweet tooth.

The 1971 German Wine Law introduced a hierarchy known as the Prädikat scale, which was based on the ripeness of the grapes at harvest—that is, the amount of sugar they contained. From lowest to highest, the classifications were Kabinett, Spätlese, Auslese, Beerenauslese, and Trockenbeerenauslese. (Between all the cumbersome names, the classifications, and the morass of regulations, trying to decipher German wine laws is like trying to master the tax code; it makes Burgundy look like a paragon of simplicity.) A lot of dreck was marketed under these headings, but the best examples were elegant, complex Rieslings with a perfect balance of sweetness, acidity, and minerality and the added virtue of being very low in alcohol, typically just 7 to 10 percent. They were some of the most distinctive, enthralling wines in the world.

But in the 1970s and '80s, German drinkers soured on sweetish Rieslings. During this period Germany saw a proliferation of French-influenced restaurants, and consumers demanded dry wines. The first wave of *trocken* (dry) Rieslings was pretty abysmal; they were often lean and harshly acidic ("battery acid" was a popular description). But thanks to better viticulture, and with some help from global warming, quality has improved dramatically in recent years, and numerous excellent dry German Rieslings are now on the market. Meanwhile, domestic demand for fruity Rieslings has effectively collapsed; German palates have been completely reoriented, and Rieslings with pronounced residual sugar are now outcasts in their own neighborhood.

David Schildknecht, who covers Germany for Robert Parker's *Wine Advocate*, humorously describes this volte-face as "bipolar Riesling disorder" and says that Germans have succumbed to "*trocken* fanaticism."

The fruity style is being kept alive, barely, by foreign consumers, and Americans in particular, which is another ironic twist to this story. Back in the 1970s, Americans were smitten with Liebfraumilch, of which treacly Blue Nun was the foremost brand. The inevitable backlash made German wines a dead category in the United States for many years thereafter. The road out of perdition was paved by two importers, Rudi Wiest and Terry Theise, who together represent a who's who of top German estates. Wiest and Theise brought in the finest off-dry and sweet German Rieslings and traveled the country preaching their virtues. These efforts paid off with the 2001 vintage, a superb year that generated enormous excitement and which created an ardent American following for the likes of J. J. Prüm, Dönnhoff, J. J. Christoffel, Dr. Loosen, Fritz Haag, and other great German growers. German wine imports to the United States have surged in the past decade, and the American market has truly become a lifeline for the fruity style. Theise told me a few years ago that if he stopped importing these wines to the United States, the producers would very likely stop making them.

Hopefully that will never happen, and those of us who enjoy Riesling can continue to have it in a variety of styles, not only from Germany and Alsace but from other regions, too. The grape does well in a variety of places. Austria produces fantastic Rieslings, both dry and sweet. Australia has had a lot of success with dry versions. The grape also has a bright future in the United States. Some appealing Rieslings have been produced on the West Coast, but the most promising American Rieslings are coming out of the Finger Lakes region of New York State, whose steep, water-facing vineyards and mineral-rich soils call to mind the Mosel Valley. Two wineries, Hermann J. Wiemer and Dr. Konstantin Frank, were the Riesling pioneers in these parts and have been making good wines for decades. They've lately been joined by some stellar newcomers, such as Ravines and Bloomer Creek, and the overall quality of Finger Lakes Rieslings has really started to soar. It has truly become a Riesling stronghold and is one of the most dynamic wine regions in the United States.

Periodically other white wine grapes emerge as possible challengers to Chardonnay and Sauvignon Blanc. For a time Grüner Veltliner, a variety native to Austria, was the new "it" grape. It was popular with sommeliers in New York and San Francisco, who hawked it as a delicious alternative to Chardonnay. Personally, I think their enthusiasm got the better of them. Grüner can yield very good wines, but for my taste it just doesn't possess much of a wow factor—certainly nothing like you find in the best Chardonnays or Rieslings. The Albariño grape from northern Spain then got hot. Albariño can make genuinely great wines— wines that can hold their own against good white Burgundies and German Rieslings. The Albariños from producers such as Pedralonga and Do Ferreiro, for instance, are sensational. However, there are also a lot of insipid Albariños, with an overbearingly tropical fruitiness—tutti-frutti would be a good way of describing it—that I find off-putting. There is just not enough of the good stuff at this point to enable Albariño to be anything more than a niche grape.

The grape that I would most love to see achieve superstar status is Chenin Blanc. Chenin is easily the most protean grape on the planet: it turns out sensational dry, off-dry, and sweet wines and can also be used to make terrific sparkling wines.

Chenin isn't exactly obscure, but it has never quite achieved the kind of renown and following that Chardonnay, Sauvignon Blanc, and Riesling enjoy. At one time it was the most widely planted white wine grape in California. But then Chardonnay took over in the 1970s, and Chenin has been an obscurity in California ever since. What's preventing Chenin from attracting a wider following? No idea. Maybe it is a tactile thing: the wines often have a waxy texture, which some drinkers might find unpleasant. Whatever the case, Chenin has never quite caught on, which is unfortunate, because it can really make some head-spinning wines.

Perhaps, though, there's some hope for Chenin. Nowhere is it grown in greater abundance than in South Africa, where it was first planted in the seventeenth century. Although plenty of Chardonnay and Sauvignon Blanc is grown in South Africa, too, the local wine industry has had particular success with Chenin in the years since apartheid ended and the industry was revitalized, and it is generally agreed now that Chenin is likeliest to emerge as the country's signature white wine. South Africa does turn out some very tasty Chenins, and as these wines gain a greater international following, it might spark some interest in other Chenins, notably those of France's Loire Valley.

The Loire, known as the Garden of France, is where Chenin reaches its apogee. A lot of mediocre Chenin is produced in the Loire, but the good stuff is as good as any white wine in the world. The Vouvray appellation in particular turns out magical wines. Domaine Huet is a legendary Vouvray producer (it was even mentioned in *Sideways*, which sent a frisson of delight down the spine of every wine geek in the theater) and makes some of the most enthralling wines you will ever taste. Huet demonstrates the incredible versatility of Chenin, crafting dry, semisweet, sweet, and sparkling wines. The three dry, or *sec*, Vouvrays, Clos du Bourg, Le Mont, and Le Haut-Lieu, are not only delicious; they have the added virtue of being amazingly affordable (around $30 a bottle) relative to the quality they offer. But Huet isn't the only beacon in Vouvray; Philippe Foreau/ Domaine du Clos Naudin, François Pinon, François Chidaine, Jacky Blot/Domaine de la Taille aux Loups, and Bernard Fouquet/Domaine des Aubuisières make outstanding wines, too, a number of which are also very attractively priced (Fouquet's Cuvée de Silex *sec* is a sensational wine, and at $15 a bottle is so cheap that one almost feels guilty buying it).

François Chidaine and Jacky Blot also make stellar Chenins in the neighboring appellation of Montlouis, whose wines display the same floral, deliciously fruity style that you find in Vouvray, along with the same chalky minerality. But another Loire appellation, Savenièrres, shows Chenin in an entirely different light. There the Chenins (they go by the name Savennières) are steely, fairly austere, and intensely mineral. I wouldn't necessarily say that they are challenging wines, but for people who like lots of perky fruit flavors, a Savennières can be something of a shock—a mineral-and-acid bath. It doesn't help that the wines take years to reach full maturity and are even then pretty austere. Jacqueline Friedrich, an American writer residing in France and the author of *A Wine and Food Guide to the Loire*, describes Savennières as "the most cerebral wine in the world," which is not necessarily a selling point in an era when consumers generally prefer the easy-sippin' stuff. But I like the elusive, almost feline character of Savennières, and the good ones can be superb. The most famous Savennières estate is Coulée de Serrant, which makes a wine from the vineyard of the same name. These days the property is famous for another reason: it is owned by Nicolas Joly, the wine world's best-known and most dogmatic proponent of biodynamic viticulture. But as I noted in Chapter Four, Joly's wines don't live up to the reputation of the estate and don't make a particularly compelling case for the biodynamic approach. If you want to taste good Savennières, look instead for examples from Domaine d'Epiré, Damien Laureau, Domaine du Closel, Jo Pithon, and Domaine des Baumard. These are all terrific Chenins and will, along with those Vouvrays, underscore why this grape deserves its star turn.

## THE GREATEST CHARDONNAYS

- Krug Clos du Mesnil (Champagne)
- Salon (Champagne)
- Taittinger Comtes de Champagne (Champagne)
- Jacques Selosse "Substance" (Champagne)
- Domaine François Raveneau Chablis Les Clos (Burgundy)
- Domaine Vincent Dauvissat Chablis Les Preuses (Burgundy)
- Domaine J.-F. Coche-Dury Corton Charlemagne (Burgundy)
- Domaine de la Romanée-Conti Le Montrachet (Burgundy)
- Domaine Leflaive Chevalier-Montrachet (Burgundy)
- Domaine Guy Roulot Meursault-Perrieres (Burgundy)
- Domaine Lafon Meursault-Perrieres (Burgundy)

## THE GREATEST RIESLINGS

- Trimbach Riesling Cuvée Frédéric Emile (Alsace—dry)
- Trimbach Riesling Clos Ste. Hune (Alsace—dry)
- J. J. Prüm (Germany—numerous wines, all worth buying; these are off-dry and sweet)
- Willi Schaefer (ditto)
- Helmut Dönnhoff (ditto)
- Keller (ditto—these are dry)
- Schäfer-Fröhlich (ditto—these are dry)
- F. X. Pichler (Austria)

# 9

## QPR

$\mathcal{I}$ DON'T KNOW if wine geeks have a greater affinity for abbreviations than other hobbyists, but we do toss around our share of them. DRC. ITB. VA. DP. RP. RO. OWC. (See the box below for the meanings.) Probably the most popular one, both in terms of usage and meaning, is QPR, or quality-price ratio. Spend any time lurking on a wine discussion board and you are apt to see this particular abbreviation invoked liberally to describe wines that are thought to offer good value for the money.

DRC: Domaine de la Romanée-Conti
ITB: in the wine business
VA: volatile acidity
DP: Dom Pérignon
RP: Robert Parker
RO: reverse osmosis
OWC: original wooden case

It is sometimes used as a backhanded compliment, a polite way of saying that a big selling point is the price. Generally, though, it is a form of high praise, indicating that a wine is not only pleasurable but also an excellent deal for the quality. QPR has become a particularly prized attribute in the years since the economy slipped on a banana peel. Consumers, critics, and retailers alike are all fixated on value these days, and even as the economy recovers, that doesn't appear to be changing. Amid the hard times, a lot of people have made a very pleasant discovery: you don't need to spend much money to drink really well.

*Value*, of course, is a relative term, one defined by your personal circumstances and the state of the economy generally. In June 2008, I wrote a column for *Slate* touting what I believed were the world's best-value blue-chip wines. I used $150 as the cutoff point, the price beyond which a wine could not be considered a value play. Suffice it to say, my timing was not ideal. The investment bank Bear Stearns had recently gone under, Lehman Brothers was teetering, and the housing market was starting to buckle. Just six months after that column appeared, the global economy was in freefall, and the article had become an amusing relic of a bygone era. Hundred-and-fifty-dollar value wines? As if! True, the market for the rarest Burgundies and Bordeaux, after briefly swooning, quickly recovered, and those wines have only gotten pricier in the years since the Great Recession hit. But the super-affluent who buy those wines are recession-proof in a way that most of us are not, and for many wine enthusiasts, the prolonged economic downturn has yielded a change in buying habits that is likely to last long into the future. People are no longer so willing to drop $80 on a Napa Cabernet or $50 on a highly rated Australian Shiraz. The sour economy didn't sour consumers on wine; it has just made them much more selective and a whole lot thriftier.

The sweet spot these days is in the $15–$25 range. You can drink very happily never spending more than $25 on a bottle. Drinking well for under $15 is a tougher proposition; there is just not a lot of compelling stuff to choose from below $15. I realize that that might not sit well with some people. A powerful strain of reverse snobbery runs through the wine world. This school of nonthought holds that big-ticket wines are mostly a lot of hype, that the qualitative difference between a $30 bottle of wine and a $5 bottle of wine is negligible, and that anyone who claims otherwise is just drinking the label.

A while back, *Slate* ran a piece by another writer saying that anyone who spends more than $3 on a bottle of wine is a sucker. The author suggested that there is no relationship between quality and price—that the difference between a $3 wine and a $30 wine is completely illusory. He cited studies "proving that our appreciation of a wine depends on how much we think it costs." He mentioned other studies showing that "laymen actually prefer cheaper wines." He said that critics might be able to distinguish expensive wines from cheap ones in blind tastings, but that's only because they have "gotten very good at sniffing out the traits that the wine industry thinks entitle them [sic] to more money." Yep, and there's no difference between a supermarket tomato and a locally grown heirloom, no difference between a McDonald's hamburger and a Lobel's porterhouse, no difference between Bud Light and Dogfish Head 60 Minute IPA. Interestingly, the author of the article pointedly refused to recommend any $3 wines, which I took to be an acknowledgment that he knew he was peddling poppycock.

He observed that sales of wines costing $3 and under have dropped sharply since 1995, while sales of wines costing $14 and over have increased dramatically, and suggested that this was proof that the public had been duped into believing that there *is* a connection between quality and price. No, the obvious explanation for these trends is that millions of Americans have become oenophiles in the past two decades, have scaled up as they have gotten deeper into wine, and have discovered that up to a certain point, the more you spend, the better you drink. People who become serious about cycling inevitably gravitate to pricier, better-made bikes; the same is true with wine. The sad reality is that there is no such thing as a great Burgundy or a great Bordeaux for under $20. The good news, however, is that many really compelling wines from many other regions can be had for $15 to $25 these days.

With most consumer goods, it is considered self-evident that price bears some relationship to quality—the more you are willing to spend, the better the product you'll get. If you are willing to spend $45,000 on a car instead of $25,000, chances are you going to get a superior set of wheels. Only with wine is the relationship between price and quality relentlessly questioned—not by wine geeks, mind you, but usually by people who have zero interest in wine and who are contemptuous of oenophiles. These are also people who are completely ignorant about winemaking, because if they knew anything about it, they would know that producing a seriously good wine requires a serious investment of money. Good vineyards are expensive, high-quality equipment is pricey, and it also costs a lot of money to farm with the kind of meticulousness that yields excellent wines. So up to a point, the more you are willing to spend, the better you are going to drink. I say *up to a point* because there is a point at which this ceases to be true. Where that point is found is a personal judgment—a matter of taste. Château d'Yquem, the most celebrated Sauternes, generally sells for five or six times the cost of Château Climens and Château Rieussec, the next-greatest Sauternes. But in my experience, Yquem does not deliver five or six times the pleasure that I derive from Climens and Rieussec, so there's no reason for me to pay that premium. (This is, of course, purely an academic point. I couldn't afford Yquem even if I did think the premium was justified!) But the idea that there is no qualitative difference between a $5 wine and a $50 wine is nonsense. Not all $50 wines are necessarily going to be to your liking, but in almost every case they will be a big step up in quality from a $5 bottle.

Regrettably, none of those regions are found in California. While a great many inexpensive wines are made in California, the overwhelming majority of them stink. This is a source of frustration for me and many other consumers; it should also be a major source of concern for the California wine industry. A lot of younger Americans are honing their palates on inexpensive imports; they have little, if any, exposure to good California wines because they can't afford the good stuff, and as a consequence, other regions are winning their allegiance. They see California just as they see Bordeaux: as a place whose best wines are meant for rich people. In offering so little in the way of good-quality value wines, California is cutting itself off from its natural constituency, from the consumer base that it is going to need in the future.

The contrast with Europe is striking. Not only do countries

such as France, Spain, and Italy offer lots of high-quality value wines; quite a few of these wines come from acclaimed vintners. For instance, Jean-Louis Chave produces Hermitages that sell for hundreds of dollars a bottle, but he also makes a delicious Côtes du Rhône that retails for about $18. Erni Loosen has an excellent $10 Riesling. Aubert de Villaine of Domaine de la Romanée-Conti, Christian Moueix of Château Pétrus, and Dominique Lafon of Domaine des Comtes Lafon, venerated names all, produce wines that are within reach of the budget-conscious. Nor is this trend confined to the Old World; Torbreck, one of Australia's finest, puts out a handful of $20 wines.

On these shores, the great Paul Draper of Ridge Vineyards has one such wine: Ridge's Sonoma County Three Valleys, an excellent Zinfandel. But he's very much an exception when it comes to top California winemakers. What's particularly strange is that now would seem like an ideal moment for an acclaimed California winemaker to emulate the likes of Chave and Loosen (or Draper, for that matter) and come out with a stellar bargain wine—something in the $15–$25 range. Producing a wine in that price range would be a shrewd way for a superstar California vintner to earn goodwill and cultivate a following among people who in the future might be willing buy the pricier stuff.

So why has no one done that? This question was the subject of a *Slate* column I wrote several years ago. Among those to whom I put the question was Manfred Krankl, whose Central Coast winery, Sine Qua Non, specializes in Rhône grape varieties and receives gushing praise ("totally profound") and monster scores from Robert Parker. Krankl suggested that one reason the Europeans were better at value wines is that they were often working in vineyards that had been family-owned for generations and that were paid down long ago. By contrast, many of the better vine-yards in California were developed or acquired fairly recently, and land in California is expensive. According to Krankl, an acre of prime vineyard on the Central Coast would cost a minimum of $25,000 and more likely closer to $50,000. When you factor in planting, farming, and labor costs, the road to profitability grows even longer. A $20-or-under wine would really be economically feasible, Krankl said, only if it could be made in large volumes. For this reason, the bargain end of the U.S. market is dominated by big players like Gallo, while boutique wineries like Sin Qua Non focused on higher-end offerings.

Krankl also said that European vintners such as Jean-Louis Chave and Dominique Lafon were in a very different position from his. Heirs to long winemaking traditions, they didn't have to build reputations from scratch; they just had to prove that they were worthy successors to their fathers. Once they did that, they were free to moonlight—to take on side projects and to carve out identities distinct from the ones bequeathed them. Sine Qua Non, by contrast, had existed only since 1994, and Krankl said his sole objective was to establish a track record of great wines—wines that could match the best of Chave or Lafon. Given the financial realities, he wouldn't be able to achieve that kind of quality in a $20 Grenache or Syrah, and it was therefore of no interest to him.

I also spoke with Ehren Jordan, one of California's most talented and versatile winemakers (full disclosure: he's an old friend). Over the years he has shown a knack for making full-throated Zinfandels but also earthy Pinot Noirs and Syrahs. Jordan pointed out that the value wines made by people like Chave and Lafon tend to come from relative backwaters; Lafon, for example, makes his cheaper stuff in the Mâcon region, not

Burgundy proper. To turn out a seriously good $20 artisanal wine in California, Jordan said, would require something similar. Napa and Sonoma were prohibitively expensive; according to Jordan, an acre of choice vineyard in either county ran $100,000 to $200,000, and grape prices were also exorbitant. But there also just wasn't much interest in Napa and Sonoma in producing lower-priced wines.

Jordan noted that in recent decades, Napa (and to a lesser extent Sonoma) had seen an influx of people who earned fortunes in other fields and who had come to wine country with a trophy-hunting mentality (my phrase, not his). Their aim was to craft luxury *cuvées* that would get big scores and become collector's items. By buying up prime vineyards and hiring fancy consultants adept at pleasing critics like Parker, quite a few of them succeeded. Among this new Napa elite, bargain wines were just not part of the equation.

Clearly American consumers are not suffering because so few good budget wines are being produced in California; the rest of the world is happily filling this void. But I think it's a pity that California winemakers have completely ceded this category to foreign producers, and I think it's particularly unfortunate that so few top American vintners dabble at the lower end of the market. Although millions of Americans are now oenophiles, wine hasn't entirely shaken its elitist image, and the image persists in part because of the attitude that prevails in places like Napa. The fact that Aubert de Villaine, the codirector of Burgundy's Domaine de la Romanée-Conti, whose wines fetch thousands of dollars a bottle, also sells a $20 wine under his own label sends a powerful message: it says that fine wine is a democratic pleasure, accessible not merely to the affluent. It would be nice if a few prominent figures in California viticulture were sending the same message.

## FIFTY OF THE WORLD'S GREAT $25 AND UNDER WINES

- Selbach-Oster Wehlener Sonnenuhr Riesling Kabinett (Germany)
- Dönnhoff Nahe Estate Riesling (Germany)
- Loosen Dr. L Riesling (Germany)
- Albert Boxler Alsace Riesling (France)
- Clos de la Roilette Fleurie Clos de la Roilette (France)
- Jean-Paul Brun/Domaine des Terres Dorées Beaujolais l'Ancien (France)
- Château Thivin Beaujolais Côte de Brouilly (France)
- Domaine Jean-Louis Chave Côtes du Rhône Mon Coeur (France)
- Eric Texier Côtes du Rhône Brézème (France)
- Domaine la Bastide (Durand) Syrah Vieilles Vignes les Genets (France)
- Domaine de la Pépière Muscadet Sèvre et Maine Clos des Briords (France)
- Domaine Pierre Luneau-Papin Muscadet Sèvre et Maine Le L d'Or (France)
- Domaine A. & P. de Villaine Bouzeron Aligoté (France)
- Catherine et Pierre Breton Bourgueil Trinch (France)
- Bernard Baudry Chinon Les Granges (France)
- Château d'Epiré Savennières (France)
- Closel/Château des Vaults Savennières La Jalousie (France)
- Bernard Fouquet/Domaine d'Aubuisières Vouvray Cuvée de Silex (France)
- Domaine Champalou Vouvray (France)

- Avinyó Cava (Spain)
- Señorio de P. Peciña Rioja Crianza (Spain)
- Do Ferreiro Albariño (Spain)
- Benito Santos Albariño Saiar (Spain)
- Guimaro Godello (Spain)
- A Coroa Godello (Spain)
- Bodegas Marañones Vinos de Madrid Garnacha Labros (Spain)
- Pena das Donas Almalarga Godello (Spain)
- Ameztoi Getariako Txakolina Rubentis (Spain)
- Sigalas Santorini Assyrtiko (Greece)
- Argyros Santorini Assyrtiko (Greece)
- De Forville Langhe Nebbiolo (Italy)
- Produttori del Barbaresco Langhe Nebbiolo (Italy)
- Vietti Langhe Nebbiolo Perbacco
- Montesecondo Chianti Classico (Italy)
- Montevertine Pian del Ciampolo (Italy)
- Isole e Olena Chianti Classico (Italy)
- Mastroberardino Fiano di Avellino Radici (Italy)
- Morisfarms Morellino di Scansano (Italy)
- Badenhorst Secateurs Chenin Blanc (South Africa)
- Badenhorst Secateurs Red (South Africa)
- Copain Pinot Noir Tous Ensemble (United States)
- Copain Syrah Tous Ensemble (United States)
- Saintsbury Carneros Pinot Noir (United States)
- Roederer Estate Anderson Valley nonvintage Brut sparkling wine (California)
- Tablas Creek Vineyard Paso Robles Patelin de Tablas (California)
- Tablas Creek Vineyard Paso Robles Patelin de Tablas Blanc (California)

- Au Bon Climat Santa Barbara County Chardonnay (California)
- Dashe Dry Creek Valley Zinfandel (California)
- Ridge Vineyards Three Valleys Zinfandel (California)
- Torbreck Woodcutter's Shiraz (Australia)

# 10

# Letting One Thousand Grapes Blossom

A FEW YEARS AGO I experienced an epiphany sitting on a barstool at a Manhattan tapas joint. I'd gone there to meet a young importer of Spanish wines named José Pastor. The twentysomething Pastor was dressed in jeans, sneakers, and a baseball cap, and with his beard, he looked more like a graduate student than a wine flogger. In fact, my first question to him was, "You're not missing class to do this, are you?" I was initially skeptical of Pastor—he looked disarmingly young, and before we started tasting, he told me that he was the ne'er-do-well of a family from Valencia and had come to the United States basically to get out of his family's hair. A dilettante, I thought—until I tried his wines. For the better part of three hours, we sampled Pastor's portfolio, and I was floored by what I tasted. The wines were all unknown to me, mostly came from unheralded parts of Spain, included some grapes that I'd never even heard of (Treixadura, anyone?), and were uniformly delicious. To say that tasting

Pastor's wines was a revelation would be an understatement. Not only had I discovered a brilliant new importer, I had discovered a side to Spanish wines that I never knew existed. In contrast to the big, oaky wines pouring out of Spain's two main viticultural regions, Rioja and Ribera del Duero, many of which tasted as if they could have come from anywhere, these were earthy, elegant, utterly distinctive reds and whites. I walked out of the tapas joint feeling quite soggy—the restaurant didn't have a bucket for us to use, so there was no spitting—but also woozy with pleasure.

You often hear it said these days that there has never been a better time to be a wine enthusiast. That's unquestionably true, and the main reason is that there have never been so many good and diverse wines to choose from. *Diverse* is the key point: the variety on offer now, in terms of both regions and grapes, is unprecedented. Wine stores are literally becoming miniature United Nations, their shelves filled with wines from once-obscure regions and previously unknown grapes. Some of those grapes have even caught the interest of American vintners and migrated across the Atlantic; alongside all the Cabernet and Chardonnay, esoteric varieties such as Ribolla Gialla and Albariño are now being cultivated in California. It's not hard to envision a future in which grapes like Godello and Aglianico are nearly as prominent as old standards like Sauvignon Blanc and Syrah. That's a very different future than many people imagined just a decade ago.

A decade ago, all the talk was of globalization. To its critics, globalization inevitably led to homogenization—less diversity, less choice. That was a particularly acute fear among some wine aficionados, who worried that the world's thirst for Cabernet Sauvignon, Merlot, Chardonnay, and Sauvignon Blanc would lead more and more producers to focus on these grapes to the exclusion of others. And certainly there are examples of winemakers uprooting less popular varieties and replacing them with Cabernet or Merlot. But many others seemed to understand that amid a worldwide glut of Cabernet and Merlot, standing out from the crowd, offering something a little different, made sense. Why become just another source of Sauvignon Blanc when you can make an amazing Assyrtiko and develop a devoted following in places like New York and Sydney? It turns out that the globalization of the wine market has actually promoted diversity, by giving producers an incentive to differentiate themselves and by making it so easy for wine to move across borders and oceans. This point should be obvious to anyone walking the aisles of a half-decent American wine shop these days and perusing the Txakolis from Spain, the Blaufränkisches from Austria, the Aglianicos from Italy, and the Trousseaus from France.

Around the world we are seeing a renaissance of indigenous grape varieties, and it can largely be credited to globalization. Take Italy, for instance. Over the past two decades or so, grapes such as Fiano, Falanghina, Nero d'Avola, Negroamaro, Arneis, and the aforementioned Aglianico have made remarkable comebacks; they may not be household names yet, but they are headed in that direction. These are grapes that might well be extinct now but for globalization, which gave individual producers and entire regions both an incentive to distinguish themselves and the opportunity to reach consumers in distant markets.

But I think probably the most exciting story in this globalized wine world is the emergence of northern Spain, which has become a source of incredible white wines. Galicia, an autonomous region in the northwest of the country renowned for its firthlike inlets and verdant landscape (it is sometimes referred to as "green Spain"), has been at the forefront of this development. At the turn of the last century, Galicia was hit hard by phyllox-

Globalization has not just been a boon for previously obscure grapes; it has also been a tonic for many small, artisanal producers. They were supposed to be globalization's roadkill, as it was widely assumed that the production of wine would increasingly be corporatized and industrialized. There has been a lot of that, particularly in California and Australia, but not nearly as much as many people expected. It's true, too, that many small producers have been hurt by the increased competition that has come with a globalized wine market. Large swaths of the French wine industry, for instance, have been suffering through a decade-long economic crisis caused in part by stepped-up competition from abroad. But here's the thing: with rare exceptions, the producers who have been hurt are ones who don't make particularly good wines. For quality producers, globalization has proven to be beneficial, enabling them to tap new markets and cultivate new clients. In fact, some winemakers in France might not be in business now but for the ardent followings that they've attracted in the United States and other foreign countries.

A good example of this occurred a few years ago when a superb winemaker in the Beaujolais region of France, Jean-Paul Brun, inexplicably had a wine rejected by the local appellation authorities. Brun owns an estate called Domaine des Terres Dorées, from which he fashions classic, lip-smacking Beaujolais, the sort that is increasingly difficult to find in a region drowning in cadaverous, insipid wines. Brun's 2007 Beaujolais l'Ancien, his entry-level wine, was rejected by a tasting panel allegedly because it had off aromas (no one else who tasted the wine, including me, found anything wrong with it). As a result of this decision, Brun was forced to sell most of the '07 l'Ancien as a *vin de table*, the lowest classification in French wine and one that permits neither the vintage nor the appellation name (in this case, Beaujolais) to appear on the label, omissions that could have seriously impeded sales. Brun was just one of a number of very good French winemakers who found themselves running afoul of their appellations, and you didn't need to wear a tinfoil hat to wonder if local jealousies were the root cause of these controversies. Brun was a fairly prosperous winemaker with a strong international following, working in an area in which many other vintners were struggling. As it turned out, Brun's international following was a lifeline after the '07 l'Ancien was demoted. Word of this calumny quickly spread via the Internet, and Brun fans in the United States and elsewhere expressed their indignation in the most effective way possible: they bought the '07 l'Ancien as soon as it became available. Score one for a globalized wine market.

era, vineyards were abandoned, and the wine industry fell into a prolonged slump. The dictatorship of Francisco Franco only compounded the difficulties. During the Franco era, Spain's wine production was dominated by large cooperatives churning out insipid bulk wines. There were pockets of excellence—Vega Sicilia, Spain's most acclaimed winery, had a number of stellar vintages in the 1940s, '50s, and '60s, and some brilliant Riojas were also made during this period—but they were a distinct minority. With Franco's death in 1975 and the establishment of democratic rule, many of Spain's cellars and vineyards underwent a dramatic overhaul. New and better vines were planted, antiquated equipment was replaced, and over time the emphasis shifted from quantity to quality.

Galicia was one of the regions that benefited from these changes. In the mid-1970s, Galician vintners took renewed interest in some long-neglected local grapes, and an infusion of financial aid from the European Union helped modernize wine production. Albariño, a thick-skinned grape said to have arrived in Galicia in the twelfth century and now the pillar of the Rías Baixas appellation, was one of the varieties given a second life. In the early 2000s, it emerged as the first big breakout star of Spain's wine boom, becoming a trendy pour in New York, San Francisco, and other American cities. Albariño remains very popular but now has some competition in its own barrio: another born-again grape, Godello, mainly associated with the inland Valdeorras appellation, has lately been generating considerable excitement.

Similar stories have played out elsewhere in Spain. In Castilla y León, the Verdejo grape began making a comeback in the 1970s and has turned the Rueda appellation into a source of toothsome white wines. For much of the twentieth century, the Basque country was a viticultural basket case. The local quaffer, known as Txakoli (*cha-co-lee*) or Txakolina, a white composed primarily of the indigenous Hondarrabi Zuri grape, was a fairly nasty garage brew produced in minuscule quantities by mom-and-pop vintners. But increased investment in the 1980s and '90s led to a big improvement in the quality of the wines, and consumer interest, undoubtedly encouraged by San Sebastián's emergence as Europe's gastronomic mecca, has soared.

Spain's renaissance has not been an unqualified triumph. In some regions there has been a move toward "international-style" wines—inky, lush reds strongly marked by new oak flavors. These *alta expresión* wines thrilled some critics but seem to have lost their charm for rank-and-file drinkers; sales have slumped sharply in recent years. And not all the white wines coming out of northern Spain are winners. Earlier I mentioned that some Albariños have an off-putting Juicy Fruit fruitiness; if I want that—and I don't—I can find it closer to home, in any number of California Chardonnays. The better Albariños, however, combine zesty fruit with bracing acidity, the same kerosene note that you often find in Muscadets, and an invigorating whiff of brine (that's the maritime influence—or the power of suggestion!—speaking). Godello tends to produce slightly rounder wines, but the fruit is balanced by a chalky, Chablis-like minerality. For its part, Verdejo is an intensely aromatic grape yielding wines that manage to be both crisp and mouth-filling; it is sometimes blended with Sauvignon Blanc, which can impart a flattering herbal note. Most of these wines are fermented and aged in stainless steel, so there's no oak influence mucking things up, and the alcohol levels are modest. These are complex but also deliciously transparent and refreshing wines.

NINE GRAPES THAT YOU SHOULD GET TO KNOW

*Mencia* This is a red grape indigenous to northern Spain, where it is found in the Bierzo, Ribeira Sacra, and Valdeorras regions. It was once thought to be related to Cabernet Franc, but that turned out not to be the case. It produces relatively light, wonderfully perfumed wines. In addition to strong floral character, the wines often have a pronounced gamey note, and the best examples also show a strong mineral edge. While a few Mencias are ambitiously priced these days, most remain very affordable, in the $20–$30 range.

*Assyrtiko* This is a white wine grape native to the Greek island of Santorini and makes what I think are the most compelling wines coming out of Greece. The vineyards on Santorini are composed of volcanic ash and pumice, and the Assyrtiko vines are trained in the shape of a basket so they can withstand the harsh winds that sometimes blow across the island. Needless to say, Assyrtiko is a resilient grape, and one that manages to maintain its robust acidity even as it reaches peak ripeness. The wines it produces on Santorini are zesty, bone-dry, and incredibly refreshing. These are archetypal Mediterranean white wines, and they speak to Greece's winemaking potential.

*Vermentino* This is another Mediterranean variety that yields lithe, crisp, summery white wines. It is the main white grape on the islands of Sardinia and Corsica and is found on the Italian and French mainlands as well. It is also turning up in California and Australia these days, which is testament to its growing appeal. The grape has some major selling points: in addition to being deliciously zesty—it is a great food wine and is particularly good with fish—it tends to show quite a bit of minerality, and it is also able to withstand hot temperatures better than some other white grapes, which is no small consideration amid global climate change. In the past fifteen years or so we've seen the triumph of Mediterranean cooking, principally Italian cuisine; it stands to reason that Mediterranean grape varieties should also be ascendant, and Vermentino is definitely a grape to watch.

*Blaufränkisch* Thanks to Riesling and Grüner Veltliner, Austria is generally known as white-wine country, but a native red wine grape, Blaufränkisch, has caught on in the past few years. A thick-skinned, late-ripening variety, it is found throughout eastern Europe (it is known by different names in several different countries), but Austria is having the most success with it. At its best, Blaufränkisch yields wines that show lots of ripe berry flavors, excellent acidity, and a good spicy bite on the palate. It is a grape that lends itself to different styles; some Blaufränkisches are fairly light and delicate, while others have a rich, robust quality.

*Godello* For the past few years, as a bit of Albariño ennui has set in, Godello has been touted as Spain's new "it" grape, and not without justification—it can produce outstanding wines. Search around enough and you will see it being compared to Chardonnay, Riesling, Chenin Blanc, and even some other grapes. Here's what we can say about Godello: it turns out wines that manage to be crisp but also a bit round and generous, a sensational yin-yang effect. Godello is indigenous to northwestern Spain, and the best examples from the Valdeorras appellation show a terrific slaty minerality to go along with the white fruit notes that predominate (think apple, pear, quince).

*Aglianico* This is a fascinating grape that yields rich, soulful wines that with their spice and herbal notes proudly wear their southern Italian origins. Aglianico was brought to Italy by the ancient Greeks, and it was apparently the mainstay of Falernian, which was the *grand vin* of Roman times. These days it is cultivated mainly in Campania and neighboring Basilicata and is considered southern Italy's noble grape, its answer to Nebbiolo and Sangiovese. The better Aglianicos show bright, zippy dark fruit, brisk acidity, and muscular (one might even say rustic) tannins. With all that structure, they can reward cellaring, but they are also deliciously exuberant in their youth.

*Lagrein* This is a red wine grape from the Alto-Adige region of northern Italy, an area bordering Austria and with a strong Germanic influence. Alto-Adige has been at the forefront of Italy's recent wine boom, and Lagrein is finally getting some well-deserved notice. It is a grape that turns out rich, highly aromatic reds that pair well with meat dishes, cheese, and yes, pizza. Not unlike Barbera, which is grown in the Piedmont region on the other side of northern Italy, Lagrein tends to be brisk in acidity but fairly modest in tannins, which helps make the wines approachable in their youth.

*Cabernet Franc* Okay, Cabernet Franc is not an obscure grape. I'm including it here because it is an insufficiently appreciated one. Cabernet Franc is the third most important red wine grape in Bordeaux, after Cabernet Sauvignon and Merlot, and is the main grape in Château Cheval Blanc, one of Bordeaux's most celebrated wines. However, Cabernet Franc's real homeland is north of Bordeaux, in the Loire Valley of France. In appellations such as Chinon, Bourgueil, Anjou, and Saumur-Champigny, it is the main red grape and produces elegant, earthy wines that go well with all sorts of food. It also yields some very good wines in Italy and California. So why isn't Cab Franc more popular? It could be the herbal note you often detect in the wine. To me, at least, that herbal note is evocative of tobacco, an aroma I love but that others might find off-putting. At any rate, I think Cab Franc produces some really exceptional wines and deserves to be more popular than it is.

*Mourvèdre* Like Cabernet Franc, Mourvèdre is a widely planted grape that deserves more respect than it gets. A thick-skinned, slow-ripening grape, Mourvèdre is believed to be native to Spain, where it is known as Monastrell. It is also found in California, where it is sometimes called Mataró, and in Australia, too. But Mourvèdre is used to greatest effect in France. It is one of the primary grapes of the southern Rhône Valley, where it is a key component in Châteaneuf-du-Pape. In fact, it is traditionally the main ingredient in what is arguably the finest Châteaneuf-du-Pape of all, Château de Beaucastel. It is also the signature grape variety in the Bandol appellation. Located on the Mediterranean coast just east of Marseille, Bandol's parched hillsides have proved especially hospitable to Mourvèdre. Mourvèdre does not suit everyone's taste. One of the grape's signature aromas is a certain gaminess—what the French call *animale*. But I think it yields sensational and very distinctive wines and is well worth a look.

# 11

# Bucket List Wines

*O*NE OF THE telltale signs that your interest in wine is mor-
phing into obsession is when you begin to feel a compul-
sive desire to experience the Holy Grail wines—the Bordeaux
first growths, the top growths of Burgundy, and the like. If you
are lurking on wine discussion boards (another indication of a
full-blown obsession), you are probably reading lots of breathless
accounts of Great Wines Consumed, and soon enough you will
find yourself salivating on your keyboard and composing lists of
Wines You Must Try Before You Die. It's a feeling I know well.
In the nearly fifteen years that I've been writing about wine, I have
chased a lot of bottles—1974 Heitz Martha's Vineyard Cabernet
Sauvignon, 1961 Haut-Brion, 1990 La Tâche, 1982 Mouton Rothschild, and the holiest of Holy Grail wines, the 1947 Cheval Blanc,
which I spent months actively pursuing and ultimately traveled
three thousand miles to taste.

The 1947 Cheval is probably the most celebrated wine of the
twentieth century. It is the wine every grape nut wants to expe-

rience, a wine that even the most jaded aficionados will travel thousands of miles to taste. A few years ago I wrote an article for *Slate* about the '47 Cheval, a piece that culminated with my one and only taste of this fabled Bordeaux. I went to Geneva, Switzerland, to try the Immortal One, and it was well worth the journey. The wine was simply amazing. The moment I lifted the glass to my nose and took in that sweet, spicy, arresting perfume, my notion of excellence in wine and my understanding of what wine was capable of were instantly transformed—I could almost hear the scales recalibrating in my head. The '47 was the warmest, richest, most decadent wine that I'd ever encountered. Even more striking than its opulence was its freshness. The flavors were redolent of stewed fruits and dead flowers, yet the wine tasted alive; it bristled with energy and purpose. It was a sensational experience, and I was also lucky: bottle variation is always a risk, and the older the wine, the greater the danger of an off bottle (because of poor storage, for instance). In the case of the '47 Cheval, there was also the risk of a fraudulent bottle; not surprisingly, given the wine's lofty reputation and price, a lot of fake '47 Cheval is on the market. But knowing something about its provenance, I'm reasonably certain that the bottle I tasted from was genuine. And if it wasn't, it was one hell of a brilliant forgery.

What distinguishes the '47 Cheval, apart from the fact that it is so mind-bendingly delicious, is that it was the product of a completely aberrant year. Nineteen forty-seven was the second of three great postwar vintages in Bordeaux, a hat trick that began with the 1945s and ended with the 1949s. Two things distinguished 1947 from those other immortal years: it was a vintage that strongly favored the right bank of Bordeaux, which is

Merlot country, and the weather that summer was almost biblical in its extremity. July and August were blazing hot months, and the conditions turned downright tropical in September. By the time the harvest began, the grapes had more or less roasted on the vine, and the oppressive heat followed the fruit right into the cellar. Because wineries were not yet temperature-controlled, a number of producers experienced stuck fermentations—that is, the yeasts stopped converting the sugar in the grape juice into alcohol (yeasts, like humans, tend to wilt in excessive heat). A stuck fermentation can leave a wine with significant levels of both residual sugar and volatile acidity; enough of the latter can ruin a wine, and more than a few vats were lost to spoilage in '47. But the vintage also yielded some of the greatest Bordeaux ever made; in addition to the '47 Cheval, there is '47 Pétrus, '47 Lafleur, '47 Vieux Château Certan, '47 L'Eglise-Clinet, '47 L'Évangile, and '47 Mouton Rothschild, legends all.

We think of excessive heat, and the drought conditions that often accompany it, as detrimental to the production of wines, and generally speaking, that's true—the grapes tend to be over-ripe, if not sunburned, and they can be woefully deficient in acidity. Yet many of the most acclaimed wines of the last century were products of blistering hot years. While 1947 was a particularly extreme case, 1959 and 1961 were also scorchers and likewise yielded a number of now canonical wines, not only in Bordeaux but in Burgundy, the Rhône Valley, and Champagne, too. One shouldn't conclude from these examples that extreme weather is *necessary* to produce truly epic wines, because that just isn't so; plenty of legendary wines have been made under "normal" conditions, too. The key point: it is very difficult to generalize about wine, which is part of the pleasure.

## CLIMATE CHANGE

To this point, climate change has actually been a boon for a number of wine regions, particularly in northern Europe. Thirty years ago, places such as Burgundy and the Loire were lucky to produce two or three good vintages in a decade, and they often lost entire crops to crappy weather. These days it is extremely rare to see a complete washout in any of these places; Burgundy hasn't had a truly lost vintage since 1994, for instance. Good vintages are the norm now, not the exception, and great vintages seem to come along every three or four years. The change in fortunes has been astonishing, and there is no question that it is due in no small part due to climate change. The growing seasons have become warmer and more consistent over the past twenty years or so, making life much more agreeable for winemakers in Burgundy, the Loire, and throughout northern Europe.

But those same winemakers will also tell you that they've been handed a poisoned chalice. Yes, climate change is benefiting them now, but in the long run it threatens to be a disaster for their regions. The weather could become too warm for the grapes they use, and they will either have to change the style of the wines they make or change grapes. Already we are seeing developments that hint at the way climate change might scramble the global wine map. In Germany, an entire category of wines has been subverted by the warmer weather. Kabinetts were once light, exquisitely filigreed, zippy Rieslings, and as such were also the most versatile wines on the German Prädikat scale. But the grapes are now coming into the cellar with such high sugar levels (a function of ripeness) that many wines labeled as Kabinetts are really, in fact, Spätleses or Ausleses masquerading as Kabinetts. Another sign of the times: In recent years Champagne producers have been scouting for land in southern England. There you find the same chalky soil that you find in the Champagne region of France, and because southern England is just a little farther north, some Champenois are eyeing it as a bolt hole of sorts—a place where they can continue to make exemplary sparkling wines if climate change undermines the quality of the sparkling wines that they produce at home.

Thanks to climate change, it is possible that a century or two from now, some of the world's most celebrated wine regions might no longer be capable of producing great wines or will have been forced to change grapes on account of global warming. The greatness of Burgundy rests in no small part on its cool northerly climate; the Pinot Noir and Chardonnay grapes ripen, but it is often a struggle to reach that point, and the fruit never gets so ripe that the *terroir* is obscured in the resulting wines. But this delicate balance is now threatened, as it is in Champagne, the Mosel Valley, the Piedmont region of Italy, and other cool-climate zones. And while it will be of no concern to any of us—we won't be around to see it—it is possible that two hundred years from now, the wines of these regions might no longer be the benchmarks that they are today, that climate change will have diminished the quality of these wines while raising the profile of other wine regions.

The only reason I've been able to taste wines like the '47 Cheval Blanc is that I am a wine writer; it's one of the perks of the job. But thirty or forty years ago I would have been able to taste most of them on my own dime; they were not inexpensive, but they were still affordable even for plebes like me. That is no longer the case. Over the past fifteen years or so, legendary wines such as these have exploded in value; the '47 Cheval Blanc, for instance, now sells for around $10,000 a bottle. With the kind of wealth that has been created worldwide over the past few decades, it was surely inevitable that prices for the rarest and most coveted wines would soar, but that doesn't make it any less frustrating. It frustrates me as a wine enthusiast, but it also frustrates me as a wine writer. I would love to see more people have an opportunity to taste these wines, and I find it very unfortunate that too often such gems end up in the hands of people who are more interested in showing them off than in actually consuming them (that's the problem with wealth—it is so often wasted on the wealthy).

So short of becoming a wine writer or making, inheriting, or stealing a fortune, what is a wine enthusiast who is eager to taste the most acclaimed wines to do? There are a few possibilities.

1.  *Attend a tasting of rare wines.* In New York, for instance, Acker Merrall & Condit, a retailer and auction house, holds lots of tastings throughout the year, and these typically feature special wines. A company called Executive Wine Seminars also puts on some fantastic tastings in New York. If you want to experience amazing Burgundies, New York sommelier extraordinaire Daniel Johnnes organizes an annual event called La Paulée; it alternates between New York and San Francisco and is attended

by many of Burgundy's finest producers. A number of events are held as part of the Paulée, and while the Paulée is not cheap, it is a great opportunity to experience rare Burgundies. A lot of fine Pinots, Burgundies and otherwise, are likewise uncorked at the International Pinot Noir Celebration (IPNC), which is held each summer in Oregon.

2. *Organize a tasting of your own.* If you have a tasting group, pool your money and buy a special bottle—a Bordeaux first growth from a good year, or a *grand cru* Burgundy with some age on it. If you don't have a tasting group per se but have some wine-besotted friends who are game to take part, you can pool resources with them to buy a rare bottle.

3. *Visit an acclaimed winery.* While some venerated wineries aren't open to visitors or are very sparing with appointments, others do welcome the general public. California's Ridge Vineyards, for instance, has two tasting rooms, one in the Santa Cruz Mountains and one in Sonoma, and both are open weekdays and weekends. While you may not get to taste any really old wines during such visits (though you could get lucky), you will get to taste current releases, and that's a treat in its own right.

## MADEIRA: THE CAUTIONARY TALE

Two hundred years ago, the most prestigious wine on the American market was Madeira, the fortified wine produced on the Portuguese island of the same name. Madeira was a favorite tipple of Thomas Jefferson and his fellow founders; it was supposedly even used to toast the signing of the Declaration of Independence. It was a wine that traveled unusually well. During the seventeenth and eighteenth centuries, the island of Madeira was a popular port of call for ships traveling to Africa, Asia, and the Americas. Before leaving, the boats were loaded with casks of the local wine, which was usually a blend of several grapes: Verdelho, Sercial, Bual, Malvasia (also known as Malmsey), and Terrantez. So that the wines could better withstand the long journeys, they were topped up with sugarcane brandy or a grape spirit, a step known as fortification. It turned out, though, that being stored in the warm hulls of ships and bounced around on the waves actually benefited the wines, producing smoother, more refined flavors. For a time, barrels of Madeira were sent out on round-trip journeys solely for that purpose. However, most Madeiras were ushered to maturity either by artificially heating the casks or by storing them in warm rooms. Among its many virtues, Madeira is surely the world's most durable wine, which explains why bottles from the nineteenth and even eighteenth century are still drinking beautifully. A few years ago I tasted a 1795 Terrantez, which was glorious; the fact that it was produced when George Washington was president was mind-boggling, and humbling.

But Madeira wasn't resilient enough to withstand the series of blows that it suffered starting in the late nineteenth century, when a combination of natural disasters (disease in the vineyards) and man-made disasters (the Russian Revolution, Prohibition in the United States) conspired to diminish both supply and demand. What had been a king among wines became a complete obscurity—it was the Joe Piscopo of wines, you could say. In the past few years there has been a revival of interest in Madeira (and rightly so—the good ones are superb), but it will surely never regain the luster that it once had.

Reflecting on Madeira's sad fate, one can't help but wonder if any of the prestigious wines of our era might suffer a similar reversal. For reasons I have discussed, it may already be happening with Bordeaux. In the United States, at least, retailers, sommeliers, and consumers have all soured on Bordeaux in recent years, turned off by the extortionate prices and a feeling that Bordeaux has lost its soul. This may be only a temporary backlash, but here's the danger for Bordeaux: because the prices are generally so high, a new generation of wine drinkers is coming of age with little exposure to Bordeaux. To these twentysomethings and thirtysomethings, Bordeaux is a wine for old rich guys, and they are finding their tasting pleasures—and their Holy Grail wines—elsewhere. Among collectors, Burgundy has already eclipsed Bordeaux, and if enough people simply write off Bordeaux, it will lose its standing as the wine world's touchstone. Top Bordeaux now sell for $1,000 or more per bottle in good vintages; could they one day sell for as little as $30 or $40? That might seem far-fetched, but if you told someone in the late eighteenth century that Madeira would fall into complete obscurity, that would have seemed far-fetched, too.

### Fifty Suggestions for Your Bucket List

- Louis Roederer Cristal Rosé (Champagne)
- Salon Clos du Mesnil (Champagne)
- Jacques Selosse Initial (Champagne)
- Bollinger Vieilles Vignes Françaises (Champagne)
- Château Haut-Brion (Bordeaux—red)
- Château La Mission Haut-Brion (Bordeaux—red)
- Château Margaux (Bordeaux—red)
- Château Lafite (Bordeaux—red)
- Château Latour (Bordeaux—red)
- Château Pétrus (Bordeaux—red)
- Château Lafleur (Bordeaux—red)

- Château Cheval Blanc (Bordeaux—red)
- Château Climens (Bordeaux—white)
- Château d'Yquem (Bordeaux—white)
- Domaine de la Romanée-Conti La Tâche (Burgundy—red)
- Domaine de la Romanée-Conti Montrachet (Burgundy—white)
- Domaine Dujac Clos de la Roche (Burgundy—red)
- Domaine Georges Roumier Musigny (Burgundy—red)
- Domaine Mugnier Musigny (Burgundy—red)
- Domaine Leroy Musigny (Burgundy—red)
- Domaine Armand Rousseau Chambertin (Burgundy—red)
- Domaine Marquis d'Angerville Volnay Clos des Ducs (Burgundy—red)
- Domaine J. F. Coche-Dury Corton Charlemagne (Burgundy—white)
- Domaine Leflaive Chevalier-Montrachet (Burgundy—white)
- Domaine Guy Roulot Meursault-Perrières (Burgundy—white)
- Domaine Vincent Dauvissat Chablis Les Preuses (Burgundy—white)
- Domaine François Raveneau Chablis Les Clos (Burgundy—white)
- Domaine Jean-Louis Chave Hermitage (northern Rhône—red and white)
- Château de Beaucastel Châteauneuf-du-Pape (southern Rhône—red)
- Château Rayas Châteauneuf-du-Pape (southern Rhône—red)

- *Domaine Huet Vouvray (Loire Valley—white)
- *Marcel Lapierre Morgon (Beaujolais—red)
- Domaine Trimbach Riesling Clos Ste. Hune (Alsace—white)
- Giuseppe Mascarello Barolo Monprivato (Piedmont—red)
- Giacomo Conterno Barolo Monfortino (Piedmont—red)
- Bruno Giacosa Barolo Falletto di Serralunga (Piedmont—red)
- Montevertine Le Pergole Torte (Tuscany—red)
- Gianfranco Soldera Brunello di Montalcino (Tuscany—red)
- Quintarelli (Italy—red)
- *J. J. Prüm Riesling (Germany—white)
- *Dönnhoff Riesling (Germany—white)
- *Keller Riesling (Germany—white)
- Vega Sicilia (Spain—red)
- *López de Heredia Rioja (Spain—red)
- Bodegas Tradición Sherry (Spain—white)
- Quinta do Noval Vintage Port (Portugal—red)
- *Taylor Vintage Port (Portugal—red)
- Ridge Vineyards Monte Bello Cabernet (California—red)
- *Ridge Vineyards Geyserville (California—red)
- Dominus (California—red)

You will notice that my list leans heavily French. Indeed, thirty-three of the fifty recommended wines are from France. Before you accuse me of being shamelessly biased in favor of

*Wines that can be purchased for under $100 a bottle.

French wines, you should know that I wrote a book a few years ago about the decline of French cuisine, a book that included a chapter looking at the woes of the French wine industry. With declining consumption at home and declining market share abroad, French winemakers have had serious problems in the past fifteen years or so, and large chunks of viticultural France are in financial crisis. Nevertheless, France continues to turn out an inordinate share of the world's finest wines. Most of the major grape varieties—Pinot Noir, Cabernet Sauvignon, Merlot, Grenache, Syrah, Chardonnay, Sauvignon Blanc, Chenin Blanc—still achieve their finest expressions on French soil. Maybe that will change at some point in the future—just as France has lost its culinary hegemony, perhaps it will lose its viticultural hegemony—but for now, the very best French wines remain the yardsticks against which most other wines are measured.

# Acknowledgments

Pity the children whose parents are working on books at the same time. While I was writing this book, my wife, Kathy Brennan, was writing a cookbook and helping to edit another. We never missed a basketball game or dance recital, but it was probably not the most enjoyable eighteen months for our kids, James and Ava. I thank them for their patience, and nervously await the payback that will surely be coming our way during their teen years, which will be arriving all too soon. I thank Kathy, too, for her encouragement and love. If a marriage can survive three books at once, it is a strong marriage, and she is a wonderful partner.

I want to thank Maria Guarnaschelli, my editor at Norton. She is a legendary figure in the culinary world, and it was an honor and pleasure to have had the opportunity to work with her. Thanks, as well, to her assistant, Mitchell Kohles, for all his help, and to Liz Duvall, whose copyediting was not only superb but also quite entertaining (a wine snob? Moi?).

I owe a debt of gratitude to my agent, Sloan Harris. He is a great advocate and an invaluable source of advice, and I feel very fortunate to be represented by him. My thanks, too, to the rest of the team at ICM.

I also want to thank my parents, John and Rita Steinberger, and my in-laws, Joseph and Keiko Brennan, for all their support, and my thanks, too, to the extended Steinberger and Brennan families.

Last, I want to express my appreciation to the wine community—to the many winemakers, wine merchants, and wine enthusiasts who have answered my queries, challenged my preconceptions, and helped make me a better wine writer. Wine is an endlessly fascinating subject, and the wine world is home to some of the smartest, nicest, most engaging people that I've encountered in my work as a journalist. I feel privileged to be part of that world.

# Index

# Index

# Index

# Index

# Index

wines (*continued*)
  connection of human experience and
    history to, 9–10
  consistency in, 45
  "corked," 38, 56–57, 58–59
  cost per bottle of, 4, 21–22, 26, 34,
    36, 44, 45, 48, 54, 87, 89, 99, 137,
    140–50
  counterfeit, 10, 44, 54–55
  damage of, 38–40, 76
  debate and argument about, 60–65,
    96
  depth of color in, 22–23, 30, 38–39,
    68, 76, 102, 119
  dirty, 79
  discount, 50
  drinking a wide range of, 21, 26
  education in, 5–6, 7, 9, 11, 15–17,
    21–41
  enzymes in, 61
  fashions in, 8, 33, 99
  feelings of anxiety and inadequacy
    about, 14–16, 18–19
  under 15 dollars, 142–43
  in 15–25 dollar range, 142
  fortification of, 168–69
  frequent drinking of, 21
  gateway, 31, 59
  importing of, 49–53, 78, 84
  maximizing pleasure of, 7, 9, 15,
    19–20
  metaphors for taste and aroma in, 6,
    15–17, 22, 24, 28–30, 63
  most desirable qualities of, 22–24
  natural, 7, 75–80
  *négociant*, 116–17, 122
  objective qualities of, 37–39

  obscure, 36
  off-dry, 92, 134, 135
  Old vs. New World, 32–34, 100, 103,
    107–9, 145
  ordering of, 36, 81–89, 91–93
  organic, 7, 77
  oxidation of, 38–39, 57, 58, 63, 78,
    119
  pairing food with, 4, 7, 67–68,
    81–93, 131
  personal discovery of, 32
  physiological and psychological
    effects of, 9, 18–20
  political allegiances linked to, 12
  possible health benefits of, 18–20
  pouring and overpouring of, 88–89
  quality in, 60, 79, 94–98
  quality-price ratio (QPR) of, 140–50
  quiet, subtle, 62
  rating and judging of, 38, 42–43,
    45–47, 66
  recommendation of, 37, 42–43, 59,
    87
  relationships and, 25–26
  romance of, 32, 53, 58, 110
  sense of place and vineyard (*terroir*)
    reflected in, 18, 23, 50, 60, 67, 68,
    96, 98–100, 102, 107, 132
  shipping of, 44
  showcasing of, 90
  single-vineyard and single-grape,
    118
  speculation and investment in,
    53–54, 114
  "spirit" of, 54
  spoiled, undrinkable, 38, 56–59, 78,
    79, 119

# Index

spoofulated, 7, 60, 61
storage of, 8, 10, 26, 32, 34, 44, 163
subtlety and complexity of, 32
sweet, fruity, 5, 91, 132–34, 135
texture or "mouth feel" of, 23, 24,
    28, 31, 34, 68, 76
thinking analytically about, 27
for 25 dollars and under, 148–50
undervalued, 55–56
value, 7, 21–22, 122–23, 140–50
vintages of, 7, 25, 36, 44–49, 54
writing about, 9, 11, 13–16, 17–19,
    24, 26–29, 33, 36, 38, 84, 127–28
wine sales:
  in big-box stores, 43
  competition in, 43, 50
  direct-to-consumer, 44
  distribution system and, 44
  in drugstores, 43
  online, 44
  regulation of, 43–44
  in restaurants, 36, 59, 81–89, 91–93
  shrewd buying and, 7, 21–22, 42–59
  in supermarkets, 43
  supply and demand in, 54, 66, 68,
    169
  wholesale, 43, 44
  see also restaurants; wine shops
Wine-Searcher.com, 45
wine shops, 7, 94
  available selections in, 4–5, 42–43,
    65, 152, 153
  browsing in, 44
  comparing prices among, 45
  competition among, 43
  e-mail offers from, 45
  point of view in, 43

proliferation of, 43
receipts from, 59
recommendations from, 42–43, 87
returning wines to, 38, 56–57, 58–59
salesmanship in, 42–43, 46, 50
shipping and delivery from, 44
temperature in, 44
wine tasting in, 42
wine snobs, 7, 13–15
  as easy marks, 10
  excesses and affectations of, 3, 4, 13,
    15, 16
*Wine Snob's Dictionary, The* (Kamp and
  Lynch), 14
*Wine Spectator*, 9, 15–16, 36, 42–43, 45,
  47, 48, 99
wine tasters, 38–41
  genetic dimensions of, 40–41
  good, 38
  "nontasters" vs., 39
  "supertaster," 7, 39–41
wine tastings, 7, 17, 26–31, 37, 48, 84,
  167–68
  for appellation designation, 106
  blind, 34, 45, 46, 94–95, 123, 142
  of Champagne, 35
  organizing of, 168
  pitting French against California
    wines in, 14, 94–95, 96, 97, 100,
    108
  in wine shops, 42
Woodside, Calif., 101
*World of Fine Wine*, 73–74
World War II, 133

Yale University, 96
  School of Medicine, 29

## ABOUT THE AUTHOR

MICHAEL STEINBERGER is the wine columnist for *Men's Journal*. Previously he was the wine writer for *Slate* magazine. A James Beard Journalism Award winner, he has written for *The New Yorker*, *Vanity Fair*, and the *New York Times Magazine*, as well as numerous other publications. His first book, *Au Revoir to All That*, was about the rise, fall, and future of French cuisine. His website is winediarist.com.